Rescue Medium
Earthbounds to Angels

Rescue Medium

EARTHBOUNDS TO ANGELS

Ros Way

Second Edition

Copyright © 2020 Ros Way

All rights reserved. No part of this publication may be reproduced, distributed, or transmitted in any form or by any means, including photocopying, recording, or other electronic or mechanical methods, without the prior written permission of the publisher, except in the case of brief quotations embodied in critical reviews and certain other noncommercial uses permitted by copyright law.

DEDICATION

First and foremost, this book is dedicated to the memory of all those that have allowed me to play a small part in their final moments of life and have enabled me to use their experiences to help others.

I would also like to thank my Guides for giving me the knowledge and experience to believe in my passion and pursue my dreams.

I am eternally grateful to my mother for her wisdom, love and support that she has given me throughout. She is my number one fan, and for that I am blessed.

I wish to thank Sue, Viv and Emily for their advice, editing and proofreading.

Most importantly, I would like to thank you, my Spirit Brothers and Sisters, for trusting this book and yourselves. We can make a difference.

If you find this book of interest, I hope you will join our
Facebook group
for support and learning about trapped souls:

Rescue Mediums Support Group

CONTENTS

CHAPTER 1: INTRODUCTION 1

CHAPTER 2: FIRST ASSIST BETTY 7

CHAPTER 3: MY THREE RED FOXES 15

CHAPTER 4: THE MAJOR 22

CHAPTER 5: JOULES AND EVE 27

CHAPTER 6: GRACE 34

CHAPTER 7: DOC AND MONK 45

CHAPTER 8: JASON 53

CHAPTER 9: VOLUNTEERING 61

CHAPTER 10: DANNY 68

CHAPTER 11: DEVELOPMENT CLASS 80

CHAPTER 12: NYAH 90

CHAPTER 13: ASTRAL PLANES 95

CHAPTER 14: MR BLACK 105

CHAPTER 15: CLASSROOMS 116

CHAPTER 16: SAMUEL 127

CHAPTER 17: CONTRACT 133

CHAPTER 18: SISTER MARIA 138

CHAPTER 19: CIRCLE 144
CHAPTER 20: NURSE CINDY 148
CHAPTER 21: ENDING 155

PREFACE

We all make soul promises when re-entering this life. Our paths are shaped, choosing those around us that will give us the best opportunities or challenges to learn valuable lessons. With the help of serendipity, things happen in the right order at the right time. Some lovingly breeze into their paths, while others may stumble, or start in the wrong direction. I, on the other hand, felt catapulted into the field of rescue work. I learned to assist trapped spirits to make their transition into the afterlife.

For many people, including me, the words 'ghosts' or 'trapped spirits' instinctively conjure up misgivings. The supernatural can be a perilous subject, dangerous to discuss and perhaps even dangerous to think about. Fear of being plunged into a parallel world with no previous training had me petrified at times. However, on the positive side, I have seen miracles occur before my eyes. I always try to keep my humility, yet feel proud of what little I have been able to offer. I feel privileged that my soul has had the rare opportunity to experience true connections with other souls, each one carving a notch in my heart.

There is more than one voice in this book. The first voice is mine, as I talk openly about how I discovered the path of rescue work. Although I have become more comfortable and confident in taking on this role, it was originally a bit daunting. I woke up one day and I realized that I was very passionate about a job in which I had no real formal training. Rescue missions came with many risks as well as numerous complications. The emotions I felt were simply overwhelming.

The second is the voice of trapped spirits. These lost souls have compelling stories to tell about the circumstances of their deaths and their decisions to stay earthbound. These can be painful and heart-breaking to witness, but they are reaching out for help. In order to tell you my story, I must tell you theirs.

The third voice is that of my Guides. It was at their request, three years ago, that I started a diary. My first task in turning my diary into a book was to try to filter through the many pages of advice given to me by my Spiritual Guides. I felt like a sort of translator, as I carefully sorted through page upon page of notes and important information. I wanted to make sure the messages that I was receiving were interpreted correctly without having to repeat anything; although some things are worth saying more than once.

The purpose of this book is to offer you the opportunity to join me on this incredible journey. I understand that each of our individual paths is unique, but I have found some commonalities and patterns that I hope will help you to understand what is happening.

As you read this book, I sincerely hope that if you feel in your heart that becoming a Rescue Medium is right for you, you will explore your own spiritual path and pursue it. I do hope that you will be touched by all facets of this book.

CHAPTER 1: INTRODUCTION

his book is not about my personal life, but I think it's important to give a picture, to help you understand me and how my mind works a little better.

I am British, born in 1969 in the Midlands. Both my parents were very heavily into spiritualism. However, as it was the 60's, many people used it as a cheap form of entertainment. Soon things got out of hand, attracting the dark side and not the light.

While pregnant with me, my mother was pushed down the stairs by a dark entity. My father walked into an invisible door, cutting his head open. Blood formed in the shape of a cross on his forehead. My mother was so frightened that it had gotten so out of control, that she walked into the first church that she found and became a Jehovah's Witness for the next couple of years.

My father continued to see spirits, but never acknowledged them. Today, my parents are not together. My mother is no longer a Jehovah's Witness, and is now a spiritual healer. As for my father, although I have tried to get him to see the beauty and benefits of connecting with the light, he just won't get involved again. He says his life has been so much quieter since he switched it off.

My mother never pushed religion or God on to us as children, but would always refer to angels, and use healing on us for minor ailments. I can recall a life-size drawing of an angel, over the bed I shared with my sister. It was something I had forgotten and never given much thought to, but it symbolises how angels protect us as children.

I grew up in a broken family. My mother remarried, and I gained two older step-sisters, as well as a younger half-brother. I got through my schooling as best I could, but never hoped to go on to higher education.

Has my life been perfect? Of course not. I, like many others, have a sympathy card that I could pull out and use if I wanted to. I never will, because life is what you choose to make it, in spite of the imperfections; I consider mine to be perfect for me. I had lots of happy memories and some bad ones as well, but such is life.

As a child, I was aware of spirits around me. Although it felt supremely natural, it was very frightening. It wasn't until my early twenties that I found God. Parents of a friend of mine were devout born-again Christians. One night, while sleeping over, I asked her father, "How do you know God exists?" He told me, "If you open your heart, one day you will have all the proof you need."

That night, as I lay in bed, I had the most beautiful experience I could ever wish for. A huge light filled me with such love, warmth and light, that from that moment on, I was convinced that God existed. It is strange: I knew that ghosts, spirits and angels were real, I never questioned that, but God, I hadn't given much thought to. I look back with wonder, as I now see that one cannot exist without the other.

I was so moved by this feeling of love, that the following Sunday I went to a Protestant church. My stepfather, having had a very cruel upbringing by Catholic nuns, was intrigued by my excitement and joined me.

It didn't take long before I knew the church wasn't for me. Some of the people came across as loving and caring yet outside of the church, I saw them as downright nasty and selfish to others. From that moment on, I decided my faith was not for show. I wanted a private relationship between God and myself. As long as I followed what was in my heart and was not told what to do via a preacher or a Bible, I only needed his approval and no one else's.

My stepfather, on the other hand, married the minister of the church and still to this day, they serve in the church.

I met my husband in my early twenties. We married and had kids, not necessarily in that order, and lived in a rented flat while unsuccessfully trying to save for a deposit on a house. Then one night I went to bingo with a few friends and won £3,500, which was a lot of money; the perfect amount needed for a deposit. I believe we had my husband's deceased mother to thank for that win.

It was our dream home, rundown but lovely. We soon found out we were not the only ones living there. Even my husband, a non-believer, who finds denial more comfortable than adjusting his beliefs, will admit that we had some non-paying tenants.

This was the start of my understanding of the spirit world. They meant us no harm; in fact, it was quite the opposite: they kept us safe. However, there was a time when my mother was babysitting and had accidentally fallen asleep, only to be woken by an invisible person tightly gripping her neck. She wasn't afraid, but never fell asleep again while watching the kids.

It was at this time that my Spirit Guide first appeared. I say 'appeared,' but all I ever saw was his feet. He introduced himself as a Frenchman named Joules. Other than that brief introduction, there was not much more verbal communication with him. I trusted his loving presence and believed in his ability to guide me through my life. He protected me and those around me. Joules stayed with me for twenty-seven years, and I was so grateful that I made a promise to him that I would pay his kindness forward.

When I was in my late twenties, I became very ill. I was diagnosed with Crohn's disease and was in and out of the hospital a couple of times. Crohn's disease is not something you are born with or you can catch. It is referred to as a twentieth-century disease, affecting the intestinal tract, from the mouth to the lower region. Although there is currently no cure, it was not life-threatening in my case.

It was in the hospital that I had my first experience of being around someone who was dying. A woman was admitted to the ward with the death rattle, a gurgling sound sometimes heard in a dying person's throat. I was traumatized by this; upset that she was alone behind the curtain but also frightened, having never been so near to a dying person. The nurses were lovely and explained that she shouldn't have been in that ward but there was a lack of beds. Instead of going home, I agreed to sleep in the TV lounge.

I had just fallen asleep on the couch, when I suddenly sensed the dying lady's presence. It was very brief, but I knew instinctively that she had just come to check that I was okay before she moved on. What a beautiful soul, she was worried about me in her last moments. I have never forgotten that night, and I still carry the guilt of not having had the courage to sit with her and just hold her hand as she passed.

In 2016, I had the chance to make up for this, with the passing of my beloved sister-in-law. We were all called in to sit with her in her final moments. I found the strength and courage not only to be there for her but to help support my family during this difficult time. I came out of the hospital very upset that we had lost someone we dearly loved, but feeling very privileged that I had been able to make it a dignified and respectful memory for everyone.

During our car ride home, my husband said to me, "I don't know how you did that, but thank you."

I replied, "If I could do that every night of the week, believe me, I would."

Little did I know that my reply would become my calling.

CHAPTER 2:
FIRST ASSIST BETTY

When Betty, my first trapped spirit, first appeared to me, it was only for a few fleeting moments of contact. Betty was a lady in her eighties, with short, vibrant silver hair that emphasised her soft brown eyes. She was warm and loving, immaculately dressed and always smiling. This put me at ease and prepared me for what was to come.

When my Guides came through a few days later and asked if I was ready to attend my first sitting that afternoon, I didn't hesitate. I believed every vigil I would be asked to partake in would be carefully selected for me by my Guides. I had never believed in coincidence and accepted everything as fate, whether that meant good or bad. Fortunately, this first experience with Betty was good.

I sat quietly on the sofa, preparing to open up and connect. My guides reassuringly watched from a distance as I was taken back in time, to play a small part in the final moments of Betty's life.

Allowing all my senses to take over, I headed to the spiritual hospital. Pulling out a piece of paper I found tucked into my purse, I read the shaky handwritten note, 'BETTY SHAW, ICU, SISTER JANE.' I made my way down the long corridor, straight to the intensive care unit. I introduced myself to a young nurse who stood at the station. "Hello, I'm Ros. I'm here to sit with Betty Shaw, Sister Jane should be expecting me."

The young nurse didn't look old enough to be in uniform; she was as tiny as a doll. She looked slightly confused, but gave a polite welcoming smile and gestured towards Sister Jane.

"Hello, Ros, thank you for coming. Let me introduce you to Betty and Edward," said Sister Jane, as I followed her behind a closed curtain.

"Betty, Edward, this is Ros. She's the lovely lady we talked about earlier."

At that point, like a sergeant major, she stomped her feet, about-turned, using the toes of her right foot and the heel of her left, and left the cubicle. She must have been in the military in a past life, I decided. Thankfully, the thought had put a warm and welcoming smile on my nervous face, as I looked at Edward and Betty.

Edward was a large man in his late eighties with thinning grey hair. His nose and cheeks were peppered with broken veins. He was wearing a dark grey suit with a not so crisp white shirt. Flecks of dandruff scattered his shoulders, a telltale sign that he had not been looking after himself for quite some time. The poor man looked like he had the world on his shoulders and at this present time, it was understandable. Watching a loved one die can be an enormous strain on anyone.

Betty, on the other hand, lay motionless, peaceful in her sleep. She had a kind face, one that reminded me of my own sweet grandmother. Her pencilled-in eyebrows and manicured nails, told me that she took great pride and care in her appearance. My heart went out to her at the sight of her tiny form, swamped in blankets.

I sat down and took hold of Betty's hand. My fingers gently studied her dry, leathery palm. Totally engrossed in my vision, I made a mental note to put some hand lotion in my bag from now on.

The energy surrounding her was weak and diminishing. I was unsure how I could be of any help, but I did not want to be merely a curious spectator who was intruding on a very personal moment. However, it had been Betty who had reached out to me, just days before. I think, even in her last days, her main concern was for her husband.

"Do you prefer to be called Mr Shaw, or Edward?" I asked.

He opened his mouth to reply but he couldn't seem to form the words. I decided to go by his first name to try and cement the relationship.

Betty slept off and on and was unable to hold a conversation. I knew she was listening to everything, and occasionally joined us by making groaning noises. I could tell whatever I had to do, I had to do this for his benefit.

After several seconds of silence, I could almost hear the gears turning in my head. I had lost the art of making conversation and needed to do something quickly. It was Edward who needed comfort and it was my job to give it.

Reaching across for the hair brush, I knocked a box of tissues to the edge of the bedside table. I stood up and began to brush her hair.

"You have lovely hair, Betty," I said, trying but failing to mask the nervousness that shook my voice.

At that moment, Edward piped up, "It was one of the first things I fell in love with when I first met her. That and her bum."

We both simultaneously burst into laughter, far more than the comment deserved. It was a release for us both. The ice had been broken.

For the next hour I listened as he reminisced, enjoying his quirky sense of humor. Edward revealed how he met his wife Betty shortly after the Second World War. I watched as he recalled a special moment with a cheeky grin on his face and a mischievous twinkle in his eye.

"She tried to play hard to get, but I used a good dose of old-fashioned chivalry, something the youngsters know nothing about that these days. I knew I was going to marry her from that very moment."

Betty made a gurgling noise, as though laughing at that comment, which put a smile on both our faces.

"We had our ups and downs. People who say they were married and it was all a bed of roses, it is just not true. But do you know, in sixty-seven years, we have only spent eight days apart?"

He lifted her hand and gave it a gentle kiss, then whispered, "Betty, remember your promise, please, my love." I could tell that was one promise he wasn't going to share with me.

I continued to listen to his fond memories of their wedding day and their family and friends. He was so sweet, so earnest and the thought of him loving Betty his whole life made my eyes prickle with tears.

By doing what we were doing, Edward and I both felt useful. Instead of just sitting there, all choked up and crying, we enjoyed taking Betty down memory lane. The tension in both of their bodies visibly melted away, bathing them in love and lifting their spirits.

Betty passed away as we sat quietly holding her hands. I watched in awe as her spirit, a beautiful iridescent blue light, left her frail physical body. In one fluid motion, she was standing behind her man, placing her soft glowing hands on his shoulders.

Her smile was infectious. I found myself beaming back at her. I didn't consider my gift supernatural, it was just the way things were. From an early age, I was accustomed to the knowledge that there were two worlds, physical and non-physical.

"Tell him I haven't broken my promise dear," it was lovely to hear her soft gentle voice.

Poor Edward: the intensity of his grief devastated me, as he looked at me with sorrowful eyes.

"Just remember, Betty would never break a promise," I whispered.

"She was my rock," he said, while wiping his face with his sleeve.

Betty tutted, having witnessed such a thing. The box of tissues mysteriously dropped to the floor. She then pulled on his collar, as if to disapprove of the crinkled shirt. I knew he had felt the slight tug and witnessed the tissues falling.

I watched as curiosity ran across his face, but he said nothing about this to me. We sat for a few minutes. A warm safe feeling enveloped the room and he seemed to gain a sense of peace. Standing up, he gave me a warm embrace. I took this as my cue to leave.

I left the vision with a heavy heart for Edward. However, thanks to Betty, I had found confidence in my new purpose.

As far as experience goes, for my first spiritual passing, I couldn't have asked for anything or anyone more beautiful than Betty and Edward. I was taught a very important lesson: that not every sitting I was to attend would always involve crossing them over. I also needed to respect others' free will. From the age of seventeen, Betty had been with Edward, and no amount of persuasion would change that. She was staying.

I like to end all of my sessions with a warm, loving sentiment like this one:

God Bless, Love and Light, Betty Shaw.

Handbook Notes

When all this started, I had no one to turn to. Information on the Internet tended to lean towards using force to ban spirits from a place, rather than using love to help them move on. My own spiritualist church never entertained the idea; not for a beginner, anyway.

I needed to learn that crossovers do not always involve showing the departed the way to the light. With that in mind, it is important that I finish each account of a passing with my thoughts on the experience. I hope that it will give you more insight into how we need to adjust to the different ways.

As I pointed out, Betty was the first person that I assisted and it taught me the most important lesson of all. When I shared my experience with a mutual friend he had wished that I had tried to talk Betty into passing over. He wanted me to reassure her that she could have come back to visit or stay with Edward whenever she wanted.

This upset me, and made me think I had failed my first task. However, when I repeated this to my sister, she replied, "Do you know for sure that if Betty had passed into the light she would have been able to return at will?"

It was an important question, and one that I couldn't answer. Had I promised that to Betty and it wasn't the case, I would have misled her. On another note, one piece of information that I didn't actually write up about Betty was that I saw no light.

You could say, as it was my first attempt at assisting a soul to cross over, that maybe I was not tuned in enough or experienced enough, but I feel that her promise to continue to stay with Edward was respected by Spirit also.

I'd like to think that you would want to respect others' free will and not just pass them over. I feel very strongly about this. With Betty, the decision to stay was made from motives of love. Despite the opinions of others, I do not regret any of the decisions I made regarding her case.

CHAPTER 3: MY THREE RED FOXES

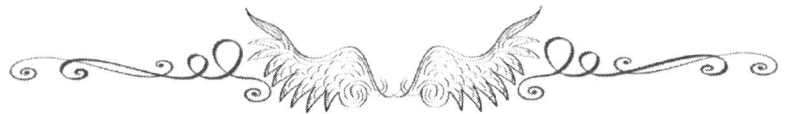

As a young child, and even into early adulthood, my fear of spirits never went away. I was able to sense them. However, the feelings were not those of pure love, as described by many mediums. I understood and accepted that I was an empath, having the ability to physically feel another person's suffering or pain. The energy they brought forth was intense. I was far too sensitive to allow communication and establish links with the spirit world.

It was this fear that led me only ever to ask for guidance from the highest and purest light, hence my connection with my Guides. None of this would have been possible without them;

they have supported me, educated me and encouraged me to spread the knowledge. They play a huge part in this book, so I need to explain how I refer to Spirit and my Guides. I would also like to introduce you to each of them.

We are all spirits, but for the purpose of this book, a spirit is a loved one or animal that has died. I hate that word, 'died,' but as we go further into the book, you will see that 'passed' or 'passing over' is a separate issue. Spirit can be good, bad, loving, naughty, trapped or still suffering.

In chapter one, I spoke about how I was always terrified of spirits. You can imagine how bewildered I felt, when one day while sitting in my lounge meditating, I watched as my spirit left my body and stood in front of me.

Attached to my arms were strings, leading to boxes on the floor. Each box had a negative title, for example: 'anger,' 'jealousy,' 'greed,' etc. Above me, connected to my head, were more floating boxes of 'love,' 'compassion,' 'forgiveness.' and so on. I knew that, at any time, I could just throw my arms up in a temper and use a negative box. The more I focused and added positive boxes above my head, the lighter and higher I could fly.

I saw a book with pictures of the human anatomy. However this time, jealousy was not in a box but rather illustrated as something that can be carried within the body. I am not sure of the full meaning of what I saw. I know it wasn't referring to my strengths and weaknesses, as I don't have a jealous bone in my body. I think it was more of a lesson that we are not born these conditions. These are either attachments that are put into or that we choose to carry around. I understand now that spirits are not to be feared. They are people, just like you and me.

My spirit stood with the same likeness as the human form but slowly transformed into a small ball. Everything within my soul, including my conscience, was in that tiny orb. This was another new understanding for me, as I had previously dismissed orbs as light, dust or reflections. I now realize how foolish I was, for not knowing that I too am a spirit.

Spirit Guides

From spirits I am going to jump, and it is a huge jump, up to Spirit Guides. These were once spirits that have experienced many lives, each one successfully mastering skills that can be used to teach. However, they are also learning to tutor, so it is not always straightforward. We will work with many guides in our lifetime, for lots of different lessons.

Guardian Angels

Above guides come Guardian Angels. Everybody from birth will be blessed with their own Guardian Angel. I feel that these are our guides' examiners, always observing from afar, and if needed they will step in. They work hard at watching our development and growth, giving us the appropriate guide or guides as needed.

for me to have a visual image of my guides. I
[...] Guardian Angel to be female. However, he or
[...] one night. It had the shape of a human body
[...] appeared as a bright light. When I asked her for her name, I was told Guille. It wasn't until I wrote it in my diary, that I was meant to spell Guille as Guyirl. I concluded that Guyirl had a dual gender: half male, half female (Guy-irl). A lesson learned.

would like to introduce you to my precious Spirit Guides.

Shamans

Before I started going to the spiritualist church, I could count on one hand my experiences with spirits, apart from my Guides. Although my family on both sides have spiritual gifts, I never considered myself able or willing to develop mine. The time was never right. I had visited the spiritualist church twice in my twenties and once in my thirties, but I found it just wasn't for me. Now that I am older, the truth is that I have run out of excuses for it not being the right time.

One night I lay in the bath hidden by bubbles and asked Joules to show himself to me. I needed to know that I was ready and able to commit. Joules never did come. However, as I focused on the bathroom tiles, an old man appeared.

He was an old man, quite unkempt. He wore a full pelt of fox fur on top of his head, the snout of which rested on his nose. His bone structure was well-defined, with elegant high cheekbones and a chiseled chin. Seconds later, he turned his head sideways and changed into a young man. He also wore the fox fur and his bone structure still matched that of the old man. Once again, turning his head in the other direction, his bone structure stayed the same, though the fox was still visible. From here, emerged the most beautiful young woman I had ever seen.

I had no idea who these people were or the meaning behind this vision, but I refer to them as my three beautiful Red Foxes. This experience had such a profound effect on me that it made me seek spiritual development from the church that week.

A month or so later, I had started a Reiki course. I was convinced that healing was the only gift I wanted to pursue.

It was my first meeting with the Reiki master who told me, within minutes of walking in the class, that I had three Shamans by my side. I had never studied anything to do with spiritual matters, although I have since learned that Native American cultures are considered to be one of the world's oldest spiritual practices.

Shamans were leaders and medicine men in their communities. They healed the injured and sick by performing sacred ceremonies, using their ability to see visions. In order to become a Shaman, there would be a series of ceremonies led by the Elders. They would be left alone at a sacred site amongst nature, where they would fast for four days. During this time, they would ask for a vision, one that would help them find their purpose in life. The natural symbols given to them such as animals or forces of nature, would then be interpreted by their Elders. After this first meeting, I did not see my Shamans again for several months.

Diary Entry 13th June 2016

I thought I was at the end of my diary last week. Nothing of a spiritual nature happened and I was questioning if I even wanted to go down this path. I had what is commonly known as a wobble. I decided to go to bed early and play a YouTube video on meditation. After three different ones, I decided to give up. I think I was trying too hard because once I stopped trying and relaxed, boy did I have a vision!

My three beautiful Red Foxes stepped forward, they took hold of my hands and we flew freely like birds. I was aware of being just spirit, a shadowy form of myself, as they and others flew around me and through me. The feeling of their energy touching mine was like nothing I could ever imagine or explain. I can only say that there was more love in that moment with a stranger, than I could possibly feel for a loved one on this earth.

I stood on top of a red, rocky mountain; the scene around me looked like something from an old Western film. In front of me was a lit campfire. The embers from the flames danced around and seemed to have their own presence.

Holding hands and dancing around the fire, I suddenly became aware of my feet. The ground was wet with dew and I could feel every individual droplet under my feet. Each tiny molecule of rain felt softer than an angel kiss.

I remember thinking how primitive we are back on Earth, and how I would be aware that the grass was wet, yet here that wet piece of grass was the most beautiful thing I have ever physically felt in my life.

They placed a white swan skin on top of my head and a badger skin over my shoulders. We danced as one with each other and the universe.

End of post

CHAPTER 4: THE MAJOR

One night, I was called by my Guides to sit vigil with Mr. Alfred Jones. I was informed by Eve, my healing guide, that he would get very upset if he wasn't addressed as 'Major.' My vision took me to his bedside to relive his final moments once again. Hopefully together we could get this right this time.

"Hello, Major."

He graced me with a smile in return, holding his hand out as a gentleman would. His grip, although weak, felt firm. I noticed his misshapen fingers, and saw that his skin was so thin, one could practically see right through it. He had a firm chin, which suggested the strength of his character.

This was the first time that I had gone straight into meeting Alfred. I wished that I had been able to have had a few previous visits to find out more about his needs prior to this, rather than only his name.

The mood of his presence was subdued and respectful. His breathing was slowing dramatically. I watched as he was drifting in and out of consciousness. Shaking his head fiercely, trying to clear his own thoughts. I have experienced many souls having a crisis of faith in their last moments, so this was my cue. Through telepathy, I was able to receive random pieces of information. They were not always consistent and complete, such as snatches of images, visions and smells. Like a psychic detective, my job was to try to piece them together. I had to either find the obstruction, reason or barrier, that might hinder a dying person from seeing the light and successfully crossing over to the divine light.

I saw body after body lining a roadside. The stench of rotting, diseased flesh filled my nostrils, nearly causing me to vomit. I had experienced rotten smells in the past, but none as vile as this. I could hear the sound of fierce artillery and deafening explosions, as bullets whistled over my head. Images of skulls and crossbones with words I couldn't comprehend (most probably in German or Japanese) flooded my mind. I quickly began to realise the significance of it all.

I was standing with him in a small room. It was cold and dark. The only light that was visible, was from the bullet holes in the door and gaps around the badly-fitting tin roof. Water was obviously in short supply, as a tin cup lying on the floor caught small droplets of water that dripped from the roof. The rough stone walls had been engraved with names and messages for loved ones. On one wall was written, in what looked like dried blood, the year 1945.

Alfred was sitting in the corner, emaciated to skin and bone, too weak to move. His breathing had become very shallow and his heartbeat had dropped rapidly. As I took hold of the Major's hand, the door flew open and a beautiful and enticing light glistened from just beyond the threshold. He was adjusting his eyes to the brightness. I waited for him to stand up and walk to God's calling, but like a deer in headlights, he didn't move; he was frozen in place. I sensed it was probably that he did not want to move. I looked down at his hand, dreadfully swollen, with deformed fingers.

I was now Alfred. I was starving and thirsty. The top of my tongue felt like it was glued to the roof of my mouth. I reached for the tin cup that I had seen earlier and swallowed the foul, sulphur-tasting water. The door had been opened and I could hear foreign male voices shouting and laughing.

Outside of the door was a plate of cold rice mixed with mud. Surprisingly, it did not bother me. I had never felt so starved in my life, and was prepared to eat anything at that point. I reached my hand out to grab the plate, only to receive a sudden vicious blow from what looked like a mallet.

My mind instantly transported me back to a memory of a family outing with my kids. We were in an arcade. I watched as one of my boys was playing "Whack-A-Mole," a popular arcade game. The object of the game is to force the individual moles back into their holes, by hitting them directly on the head with a mallet, thereby adding to the player's score. I withdrew my hand rapidly. Thankfully, up till now, I had never felt physical pain during my shared visions.

"Bastards!" I shouted, hoping I hadn't said that out loud. 'Barbarians' was too soft a term. These sick people were using meal times as their form of entertainment. I could fully understand now why Alfred was afraid to leave his cell. My sixth sense told me that the guards would often leave the prisoners' doors open, daring them to escape. They took great pleasure in torturing them, like a twisted game of cat and mouse.

Suddenly I was once again in my own body, looking directly into this brave man's eyes. I needed to earn his trust. I took advantage of one of my few gifts, which is the ability to put people at ease. Everything in the room, including Alfred, was in black and white. I was standing with the light behind me, radiating around my body. He stared at me like he was looking at an angel in full color.

Keeping eye contact and a loving smile, I walked backwards, holding his frail hands and drawing him with me. As I stepped over the threshold, I stopped and waited for him to gain my trust. Suddenly, we were flying; we had both flown out of hell.

Back in my own room, I heard a faint, "Thank you." I was sure that it wasn't my imagination.

God Bless, love and light, Major.

Handbook Notes

I was once shown a very simple vision of an old lady packing up her home to move. For a brief moment we went back in time. I witnessed her lift up the rug in her lounge and simply sweep the rubbish underneath. On the day of her move, as she was moving to Heaven, a metaphor really, she picked up a corner of the rug and was suddenly overcome with the same memories that she thought she had disposed of long before.

I feel strongly that this also connected to the Major. There is an important lesson to be learned here. Never sweep or hide traumatic events in your life out of sight. The traumatic events pertaining to the Major were the reasons why he prevented himself from moving on.

Sadly for the Major, he lived in a stiff upper lip age. He had buried his torture so deep that this could have haunted him for a long time, had we not been blessed to meet.

CHAPTER 5: JOULES AND EVE

Joules was my first Guide; the one that I was aware of in my twenties. He stayed working with me for nearly thirty years. I never saw Joules in person; all I ever saw was his two feet in sandals. He supported me, warned me and kept me safe, without really ever having a conversation.

The easiest way for me to work with Joules was to understand that he was my intuition. Knowing and living with my intuition allowed me to keep my religion and beliefs to myself.

Trusting him to give me signs, such as the feeling of a strong sensation in my back, when I needed confirmation to support a thought, allowed me to build up a great deal of love and trust. It was only in March 2016 that I was able to have a two-way conversation with him and bless him. Once that doorway opened, I have never stopped asking questions since.

Joules' first words:

"One can live life to the fullest without acknowledging spirit by your side. We are here to enhance your life, to guide you and support you on your journey. Not all life's lessons will be made clear to you; just being the love and light that you are can be a privilege on its own.

Everybody has the potential to connect our many worlds together, allowing not only ourselves to grow, but in doing so, allowing the universe to heal.

Our worlds, although very united, can be very divided. By dividing, you can live your life, feeding your soul and others that you connect with. United is when we start to make changes, healing the wounded and ending all suffering.

This is a huge task, overwhelming and lonely at times, If you wish to participate, however, that being said, before entering this life, you made your life promise to God. Neither path is right or wrong, as love and light will flow from you, healing and nurturing those in your path, without you needing to be aware of it.

Embrace us when you feel the time is right."

—Joules

Needless to say, I embraced him instantly and asked a question. I had been troubled by how I was being judged for having materialistic things and a business mind, it was then that I heard a voice saying:

"I curse the Bible at times, allowing many to take words literally. Money is the root of all evil is a perfect example. Just one missing word can lead to much confusion.

Attachment, that is the key. It is one's attachment to money that can be the root of all evil. Yet should your attachment to it be healthy, then why shouldn't you be blessed with the fruits of your labour, valued in your world?

Wealth and success can be just another lesson to some, given and taken away, or never given at all. Some may be rewarded in other ways, some may be tested given to as a tool, in an exercise of value."

—Joules

As you can imagine I was jumping for joy, not because of the clarity he shared with me, but because I could hear him. I thanked him for being with me for so long and asked him another question. I knew heaven was beautiful, who didn't, however, nothing could stop me from worrying about being physically apart from my loved ones on this earth.

Being extremely honest, I had often thought it would be easier, less painful, if I had no faith. Once I was dead and buried I couldn't feel the pain of missing my kids. For many spiritual people it would be so easy to repeat the words that time has no meaning there, but you are talking to the hardest critic, who needs proof and a clear understanding to make sense of things. It was then that I was shown a vision that ended all my fears. I will share this with you in a later chapter.

I had a bond like no other with Joules. He taught me a lot. It breaks my heart still, months later, that Joules had to move on. I was told by a medium once that they never leave you, but I know a goodbye when I hear one. I miss him terribly. This is a post from my diary when Joules said his last farewell.

Diary Entry 19th July 2016

I am hoping I had a dream last night and not a vision. Yesterday I spoke too soon, worried that I had had no contact with Joules or anyone for the last two weeks. I went to bed, unable to sleep, mainly due to the heat. I decided just to have a one-way conversation, in the hope that Joules would hear me.

It has been a terrible few weeks. Within a few days, I had lost my sister-in-law and I had to support my friend as we cried, watching her dog being put to sleep. I was also told of yet another family member passing.

I felt alone in all this, abandoned at my hour of need by the one person I relied on so much: Joules.

I knew of the famous quote: 'Footsteps in the Sand,' but that wasn't cutting the mustard with me. Joules has taught me so much, I have been privileged, not just to have my Guide join my world, but for him to take me to their world, such a huge thing for anyone and at this moment in time, all I needed was to feel him near. All I asked for was a cuddle, and yet it didn't come.

That's why I had to apologize, because I was angry at him. I felt like he had abandoned me when I needed him the most, but in truth, although I never felt it was right, I was left to feel that way. I had to apologize for thinking so little of him and accusing him of not being there. It broke my heart more than if I had hurt him with my anger.

My first words to him were that I was "Sorry," and by saying it, I knew my heartache had lifted. Suddenly, there he was in full form, sitting on a picnic blanket, in the middle of a beautiful field. No longer appearing as just two feet. He was smiling, as I walked up to join him.

I could see his face, the same face I had seen in a picture overlooking my shoulder once. I sat with him and said nothing, but listened as he explained the following:

"My dear child, I have been by your side for thirty years, waiting for this day. I am filled with pride as I watched you grow, shine and graduate and now become the beacon that you are.

I can take you no further, so with love I must now leave you. If I could have thirty more years with you, my angel, I would do so in a heartbeat. Make me proud."
—Joules

He looked to his left, and I followed his gaze to see a lady walking towards us. He didn't say anything about her, but I knew that she was to be my new Guide. He stood up and walked away. I never said a word. I knew that it was Joules' job to get me on a path of belief and working for spirit with no turning back. I felt so proud of him, that he too had completed his task.

I looked at the lady standing in front of me now. She had a lovely white soft glow about her, she had long black hair tied up in a bun and brown eyes. She was slightly taller than me, I would say about five foot seven inches, and carried a white rose in her hand. She didn't tell me her name, but I have since learned her name is Eve.

"You have so much to learn and our journey together is going to be a hard one, but don't worry, my love, as we have already given you a taste of what is to come and as expected, you passed with flying colours. You are ready, but first we need you to do your homework. Your building blocks are there, but the cement is not dry. Seek your answers. We have given you the people around you to help. Never dismiss a chance meeting or conversation with a stranger. You will be sent many a lesson, by many different ways, and you must learn to trust your own instincts now, as they will not let you down.

Look at the rose carefully, what do you see? Beware of things, study the details that will keep you safe. Your beacon is bright, your heart is trusting and you attract many spirits excited to join your energy. Both Terry and Peter were right; the safety is in the details."

—Eve

Peter was the tutor at the church I attended and Terry was a spiritual friend. I studied the rose in her hand; at first sight, I had thought it was white as she walked up, but as I looked again, I could see it was like glass, see-through, with a long stem and no thorns.

That was the vision over. I know it is exciting, but I am trying to feel sad about losing Joules, but I can't find the emotions. I will take it as a blessing that I had him in my life for so long.

One thing slightly worries me and that is what is to come. She said it was going to be a hard one; I worry that things might turn bad for me in this life. It's funny, but Peter said exactly the same thing, so I will speak with him as soon as possible.

Since working with Eve, things did get very tough. Eve is more of a healing Guide to me. Unlike Joules, she won't talk to me very much and certainly won't pander to my worries: she is very much a tough love tutor. She reminds me of Nanny McPhee: "There is something you should understand about the way I work. When you need me, but do not want me, then I must stay. When you want me, but no longer need me, then I have to go."

End of post

CHAPTER 6: GRACE

A phenomenon widely reported is that people who are facing death often undergo profound life review experiences, reliving their life history in chronological sequence, and in extreme detail.

This was not the case for Grace, although I would like to think that her life memories passed before her once she was on the train.

Above Grace's bed hung a beautiful yellow butterfly. A few years ago a family friend was in hospital, and it was there that I had learned about the butterfly scheme. It was being widely used across the UK to discreetly notify staff, in a simple and practical way, that the patient suffered from memory impairment, or in her case, dementia.

As I connected, my heart went out to her. Grace's illness had taken its toll on her. Her deep wrinkles, grey thin hair and sunken eye sockets, were sad to see, yet I felt a deep connection, forming an instant bond as though I had known her all my life.

"Are we ready?" she asked.

In spite of her dementia, she seemed quite alert, and smiled warmly. I hadn't even introduced myself yet, but I had been trained that it was best never to question or correct, but instead, to listen and try to find the meaning in what was being said.

"Yes, Grace. I'm ready when you are," I said, returning her warm smile whilst taking hold of her hand as she lay in bed.

"We must hurry, the train will be here soon," she spoke excitedly.

"Where are we going again, Grace?" I was both fascinated and curious by this conversation. Many people begin to speak in metaphors about a journey, as though announcing their own departure. Little did I know her vision would be such a visual treat of the yesteryears.

Grace and I stepped into a picture-perfect train station, a scene set somewhere in the 1950's. Grace bought and paid for two tickets, and handed mine to me. It reminded me very much of a large raffle ticket; I slipped it into my pocket.

As we stepped onto the platform, a railway porter, pushing his wooden trolley, tipped his hat and smiled. He offered to take Grace's case, but she politely declined.

Women and children of all ages were impeccably dressed in summer pastel colours and well groomed, wearing coordinating hats, shoes, and handbags, as though they had just stepped out of a Vogue fashion magazine. The gentlemen represented perfect images of family men, breadwinners, with their trilby hats and smart business suits, all in conservative shades of grey, blue and brown. A few of them were wearing trendy overcoats, still highly fashionable today.

We sat on a lovely wooden varnished bench, the pleasing fresh smell of flowers captivating yet another of my senses.

I giggled at the old advertisement boards hanging on the wall. A man sat smoking his Woodbine cigarettes, as his wife smiled, removing his shoes. A glamorous housewife still wearing her apron, proudly holding a box of Omo washing powder, displaying its slogan, "Adds brightness to whiteness."

How times have changed since the 1950's. It was a wonderful era, many say, they were on the threshold of many wonderful inventions, but it was also the decade that saw the last of chivalry.

Turning my attention back to Grace, I saw that in contrast to the beauty around us, she was wearing a floral full-length nightie and a matching dressing gown. Her face was pale and her hair needed a brush. She didn't seem to mind, so I averted my eyes, as not to bring her attention to it.

Her sights were fixed upon her light tan leather case. It had character, each small scratch and dent adding to its history and charm. Suddenly her smile faded.

"Oh my goodness, I haven't packed," she cried, using both hands to open the double-locking clips.

"I've forgotten everything; it's been taken from me. Oh my, please help me, Ros."

It felt strange. I couldn't recall telling her my name, but regardless, I had to help. Clarity came, and I knew exactly what I had to do. The empty case she referred to was another metaphor. For a second, I'd thought she was referring to her clothing, but in fact, she had meant her life memories.

Out of nowhere, two of my guides, Doc and Monk, appeared on the platform across from us. I watched as Doc's gaze lowered and seemed to focus on something underneath our bench. I reached down and took hold of what felt like a large heavy book.

I have never questioned how things just appeared in my visions, but thankfully they do. As I pulled it out and placed it on my knees, to my shock and horror, it was my photo album, not hers, what on earth would I need this for? I felt deflated as I looked up to see Doc and Monk, smiling and nodding.

"Who is this, Grace? Is this you?"

I pointed to the picture of myself taken at the age of six. She looked closely at it. I wasn't deliberately trying to mislead her. It felt as if what I was doing was dishonourable, yet I only had my own album. I would have felt more comfortable if I had been given the Queen's photo album.

Extreme memory loss, in some cases, can cause people to not recognize those close to them, or even recognise their own reflection.

"Yes," she said. "Look, I had blonde hair then," she added, excitedly.

I pointed to the picture of my two boys playing on the beach. "Who are they, Grace?"

"Those are my two boys. That was taken just before my son got stung by a weever fish."

I could relate to that memory, having experienced it with one of my own children.

Carefully, we went through the album, with Grace seeing herself in my place in every picture, from being a child with my parents and then as an adult with our boys growing up. I made sure I never gave too much information away or asked too many questions in case her memory came back, and she realized I was misleading her. Going through each page, I began to see her looking younger, the worry lines disappearing, as she radiated with the love of being given her life back.

We reached the last few pages, which were filled with photographs of my wedding day.

"Grace, look." I paused to see her reaction. "Look how lovely you are in your wedding dress."

I blushed, as I was obviously referring to myself and felt uncomfortable.

"I wouldn't quite say that," she mocked. My hot cheeks must have been beetroot red.

"That's my husband, John," she said, pointing to the man I had married, whose name was also John; a very common name, so I supposed it was a coincidence.

"Let's pop this into your case Grace."

At the back of my mind I worried if I would still have my album at home and if I had just given away my life memories.

A picture fell on the floor; it was a recent picture, one that had been taken of a group of my very close friends. She picked it up.

"This is Pauline, Brenda, Tina and Lisa," she said, pointing to each in turn. I was dumbfounded. She had just given the correct names to the correct faces. How could she know that? She knew things I hadn't told her; it was far more than coincidence, now.

Quietly, I contemplated the situation. I had just shared with her all my precious memories. Don't get me wrong, I loved the fact that I had the chance to reminisce, but I had a sudden thought that in fact, this must be the beautiful moment, when one sees their life flash… I couldn't even bring myself to finish the sentence.

"Tickets please," a guard shouted, as he walked up to us. Grace handed him her ticket, and he snipped it, smiling. "Nice to see you, Grace. Your train is due in three minutes."

Then he turned to me with a cheeky grin on his face. "Tickets, madam," he requested. Overwhelmed with unfamiliar emotions, I sat frozen, unable to speak. *Not bloody likely* were the words that crossed my mind. I felt like I was holding a hand grenade with the pin pulled out.

My body reacted to the sudden shift from feeling in relatively good health to the threat of a death sentence, and I clung on to the bench for dear life.

My brain might have been a little slow on the uptake, but it was kicking in now. Was I... dead? The word hung above me like a guillotine, ready to fall at any moment.

How did Grace know my name? How did she know my husband's and friends' names? Was I Grace, was that it? I had felt a familiar connection with her right from the start; maybe I was seeing my future? Come to think of it, since turning forty, I had had occasional fears that I had dementia, but after listening to my friends going through the same things, I had assumed being forgetful was just normal at my age. I should have gone to the doctor. No, No, I can't be Grace; why would she have bought me a ticket?

My concerns were soon chased away by self-preservation and the instinct for survival. My heart pounded in my chest. Mentally I set the wheels in motion and ran through my escape plan. I looked for the exit signs; there were none. That's okay, I thought. I would run back through the entrance, as I could see the sun's rays filtering through. Yes, that's what I was going to do. Then I remembered the Heavenly light.

" No, the light, Oh, you nearly had me then." For a moment, I chuckled at my own dark sense of humour, then felt my shoulders slouching in defeat. "That's it, I am stuck."

I couldn't risk running to the light and I dared not get on the train. I was trapped in God's waiting room. *How ironic is that? Some advocate I am*, I thought. I passed people over to a better place, trying to take their fears from them, and yet, here I was sitting, glued to the bench, refusing to move. It wasn't because I was frightened of dying and going back to my spiritual home, but because I was too young, and I hadn't had the chance to say my goodbyes.

"Madam, can I see your ticket please?" the guard said again, laughing, and his wide smile made my stomach flip. I felt the blood run from my face, my insides all shriveled like a deflated balloon. My fingernails dug into the bench. The underside was unvarnished, and my nails penetrated the soft wood.

Really, brain? I'm fighting for my life, and you want to register that detail? I thought. *If I get out of here, I'm seriously going to think about taking you to a psychiatrist.*

I eventually convinced my rigid left hand that it would be safe to let go of the bench, as there was no way I was getting on that train, ticket or not. Like a child, I held out the ticket at full arm's length away from him, but, reminding myself I was not a child, I managed to muster up enough incredible self-control to prevent myself from throwing a tantrum, kicking and screaming.

"Thank you, madam. Platform only." He gave a wink and went on his way, laughing.

I looked at my ticket, and there it was in large bold letters: PLATFORM ONLY. I didn't know whether to laugh or cry; that really had been too close for comfort.

The steam train made its grand appearance, sooty smoke billowing from its engine. Grace stood up and bent over to give me a cuddle, yet it wasn't Grace from the hospital, wearing a dressing gown; this lady was stunning, a real-life Grace Kelly.

She hugged me tightly. "Thank you, Ros, for giving me my memories back."

The uneasy moment had passed now. Suddenly, I had a new perspective on life that I had never achieved before. I knew that the very essence of life was a gift, even though it had come at a frighteningly heavy price.

"My case is heavy," Grace remarked.

My good manners wanted me to carry it onto the train for her, but I still couldn't let go of the bench, just in case.

Once settled in her carriage, Grace pulled down on the leather strap, lowering the window. "By the way, Ros: you were a beautiful bride, and still are. God Bless, love and light."

Handbook Notes

Grace has always troubled me, as I had no option but to mislead Grace into thinking my photo album was her life, that she had got upset about losing. In the moments of connecting with lost souls and entering their vision, I have no time to plan things: it all takes place in the immediate present. I had no idea what was under that bench and even if it had been the Queen's photo album, I would have had no choice but to have done the same thing as I did. One thing I don't think I have made clear is that, when using the word 'I' in describing the crossings, I should really use 'We,' as it is both my Guides and I who are involved.

Very early on in my writing, I joined a writers' group to help get feedback on my work. Having shared my story of Grace with the group, I was hurt by one woman's judgmental comments of evil undertones and moral wrongs. This cut me so deeply that I stopped writing for months and struggled to go back to it. I have no problem with criticism, if it is given as constructive criticism to help me.

Upsetting comments are the very reason I questioned putting my name to this book. I have insecurities, mainly about being judged as either a liar or an egotist. Writing this book, I found that this woman's comments were something I needed to learn to rise above.

So, what was the lesson to be taken regarding Grace? It was confusing to me. I wasn't sure whether I was the helper or whether Grace was doing her final task in teaching me things. On a crossover point of view, I did mislead Grace by giving her my memories, as I wasn't given her own memories to remind her. My view is that, although it would not have been right to mislead Betty, as she had a healthy knowledge of her intentions, for Grace, it was necessary to make an instant decision as we went along, and I feel my decision was right for Grace..

CHAPTER 7:
DOC AND MONK

*I*t was in one of my meditations that I met Doc and Monk. Sorry, I have no names for them and don't wish to try to force any. Standing in front of me was a doctor; I would say he was in his eighties. He wore a dark three-piece suit and by his foot stood an old-fashioned doctor's bag. Facing him was a monk, also in his eighties, wearing a brown habit with a tan rope belt around his waist.

In their hands they held playing cards, not like the usual playing cards; hearts, spades, diamonds and clubs. These pictured real people, similar to 'Happy Families' playing cards.

Doc spoke in a firm voice, "*I will take this one and give you that one,*" as he pointed to the cards in Monk's hand.

I have never in my life lost my temper as quickly as I did at that instant. I wrongly assumed that the doctor was choosing who to help, and the monk was choosing who died.

"How dare you, who are you to decide who lives or dies? Only God has that right," I screamed at them both, with intense anger. I wasn't sure where this streak of bravado had come from, but I was disgusted with them.

At that very moment, I flew backwards from my present sitting position, at such speed that I'm still not sure if I had purposefully backed away from the situation, or if I had offended them both and was physically forced back. The next thing I was aware of, in my vision, was being brought slowly back to the table.

I saw Eve standing at the side of them; she walked behind me and placed her hands on my shoulders. As she did so, I found myself gasping for air; I wasn't sure how long I had stopped breathing for, as my awareness took me back to being laid on my bed. I took the biggest breath of my life. I think I had returned from my meditation far too quickly; not the healthiest thing to do.

Once Eve had calmed me down physically, I re-entered my vision. I noticed that I had five cards placed in my hands. The headings were different on each card and the pictures under each one were of people in my life.

- HEALER – There was a picture of my Mum.
- FRIENDSHIP – This was a picture of Sue, a very close spiritual friend, who believes and encourages me with this book.
- TEACHER – This was a lady who was head of the Spiritualist Church that I attended.
- COMMUNICATIONS – This was a woman, a good medium, whom I admired at the church.
- ANCHOR/ GROUNDER – This was Terry, a wise older man I had also met in the church.

All these people were ones I had sourced, to help me realise my spiritual path and to allay fears that I had, giving me a good support system should I find myself in difficulty. I looked upon Doc now, as part of the team, needed in my crossing overs, offering help with troubled and painful passings. The Monk, on the other hand, became involved in peaceful spiritual passings.

I felt ashamed to have jumped to such wrong conclusions, but I am only human.

Doc spoke: *"You have now been dealt your hand. Your search for self-protection may not be your best ally. Your answers do not lie with others at this time; look within, for there lies your protection."*

Once again, looking back down at my cards, I noticed that they had all changed, all the pictures were of me now, under the same five titles. When my vision was over, I realised that I indeed had the skills to be all those people, I was in fact, equipped to help those in need from the spirit realm.

Penny

I decided to write about the crossings I had experienced in much more detail than my diary posts. I wanted to take you on the journey with me, for you to experience all the emotions that I felt. This is where Penny, a new guide, came in. I haven't met her visually. Penny and I wrote up the experiences, and I read them with such pride. I don't hear Penny in my mind, but if I pick up the pen, her words will flow.

At first, I struggled to write this book. I questioned why I felt unable to talk about myself, as my greatest fear was being judged as egotistical, yet I have claimed no extraordinary powers in spiritualism. I am lucky if I can read a flower, to give someone a message. I could not understand why Spirit would not ask someone else with more experience or perhaps someone with a gift for writing, to carry out their request. This was Penny's lovely answer:

"You are but the pen. It is the pen itself and the person in front reading the ink that matters most. You ask, why you? You shine bright, my love, but no brighter than anyone else. It is the conviction, truth, and knowledge in your heart that will light this new path. We have a universe of our beloved lost ones, a task so great that shadows your world and dims our hearts. We are reaching out for help; little can be done by one alone. You have been given the

pen that will guide you in our quest. Fear not your own thoughts, for allowing oneself to be judged is to judge oneself.

You fight for us with bravery and the truth will win. Remember, you must pass on, not what you have received, but what God's guidance has shown you. Let that be the only thing to be judged in your mind if you must, for judged it will not be. The pen will guide you forward; your voice will carry this message far. Blessed are those that not only listen, but are brave enough to follow guidance. Be brave, my tadpole, be brave."

—*Penny*

The tadpole was a little joke between us, concerning a vision I had been shown a few nights before. I was sitting in the middle of a group of people, who had come to advise; these were my Council of Wise Men. They were huge in proportion to me, making me feel no bigger than Tinkerbell. In the middle of the group stood a glass bowl, with what seemed like the energy of the universe inside it. It's hard to recall what it looked like, as it was more of knowing what was inside, than actually visualising it.

I along with many other people were little tadpoles. We spent hours swimming around the bowl, constantly banging our heads to find an exit. I watched as we all tried without giving up. It became clear to me that all I needed to do was to take a huge leap of faith and swim higher, so that I could exit the top of the bowl and be reborn. I needed to raise my awareness and vibrations.

When the vision had gone, I blushed to realize I hadn't been a tadpole at all, but a sperm. I have let the private joke out of the bag now!

Guyirl

The second time I met Guyirl, my Guardian Angel, I was in bed, listening to a meditation on how to connect with your own Spirit Guides. I tried hard to relax, to follow the instructions on the video, and to walk down a path that forked, through meadows until a mountain appeared on which my Guide was supposed to stand. I was not doing very well and was just about to call it a night, when Guyirl actually appeared.

I lurched forward in my vision, running as fast as my legs could carry me, all I wanted to do was jump into the arms of my Guide, but as soon as I leapt up, I awoke, I came back from my vision, lying in my bed. I tried hard to return to the vision, but the video was ending, talking about bringing oneself slowly back to the present. I couldn't get back into my vision, so I picked up the pen and paper on my bedside table. This is what I wrote:

"Oh, wise one, how you seek knowledge has caused quite a stir here. I need to explain my state of being with you from experience. I have lived many hundreds of lives on your earth, gaining knowledge and life lessons to be where I am now. I have had fame and fortune above and beyond my needs and yet these were the saddest of lives I lived. My last life was consumed with grief, not

only of my fellow men, but for humanity as a whole. It was this life that I felt complete and rich within, beyond any measure.

I graduated, as you like to put it, to be here now, guiding you in your life lessons. I cannot, like you think, use my experiences as answers to your problems. I can guide, steer and place people in your path, but never use my knowledge as your solutions. As you rightly know, I am your guardian and eagerly long for your attention to guide, however, we have now gone above and beyond our expectancy of insight. You no longer see me as the human form most wish to see and seek to not only touch, but embrace my presence and knowledge; for this I have had to seek your team of councillors.

Decisions have not been made as of yet, as reaching out to us is a blessing, used by many, reaching out to us, to go beyond a touch and holding hands is quite a responsibility and a privilege to be asked. However, like the starling you are, you have asked for an embrace. Although I glow with pride, I am unsure that such vibrations of energy can be consumed by your five senses alone. In council, we discussed whether this could be possible and what repercussions can come from this. We must wait for the verdict."

—Guyirl

I didn't have to wait days or weeks for the verdict; as you can imagine I was on cloud nine. It was early in the evening, so I ran downstairs to ring my mother with this exciting news, however, I hadn't got to the bottom of the stairs before I heard the words *"Pick up your pen."*

"It has been decided that I can only talk you through our embrace. This is new to me. How do I explain my very existence, when all I feel is an existence? It would be like you trying to explain to an infant how your organs work, without prior knowledge of biology. Your Shamans blessed you with both, feeling a vibration of a raindrop, and privileged you with interconnecting with spirit to spirit.

Think of us as a symphony, an orchestral piece made of many notes. Each note carries notes within notes. Now imagine you have no hearing; it is quite possible to experience feelings and emotions through your body by just the vibration of one note, however, tuning into notes within notes is not physically possible within your senses on earth. Yet you felt the thousand molecules within one drop of rain. Now, understand that what you felt then carries information, not just feelings.

We are too complex to understand. Each vibration or note contains memories and lessons through thousands of years. You are not even capable of dreaming the wonders that await you, and nor must you, for one cannot appreciate the vibrations of beauty around you. You are still very primitive in your understanding. By blessing you with the true knowledge we must not lower your insight into the beauty that surrounds you and leaves you longing for God's true beauty here. I know your innate soul understands all I am trying to teach you. I have been given permission to embrace when I feel the time is right for both of us, until then I send you a loving embrace."

—*Guyirl.*

CHAPTER 8:
JASON

As I walked down to the A&E department, with Julie, one of the nurses, she passed on the little information she had just received. A young man had just been brought in with serious burns, which might possibly prove fatal. His poor distraught wife was upsetting the other casualties with her hysterical cries. I could feel the sense of urgency rising with every step that I took.

As we pushed through the double doors into the spacious white room, I was hit with the weighty silence in the air. I knew it was going to be bad... Suddenly, I was in a heightened sensory mode. The tension in the room was thick. It was mental chaos;

the room had a fog of sadness and worry to it. A super-strength reek of putridity in the air made sense as we walked closer. There was a faint smell of antiseptics that I tried to concentrate on, as the food I'd eaten earlier threatened to surface.

Six firemen, wearing their high visibility jackets, stood either side near the doors, speechless, awaiting news. I could hear their silent prayers as we passed. Then I heard the hysterical screams, coming from the distance. I needed all the inner courage I could muster and called out mentally for Doc and Monk to come.

"Are you sure you are up for this?" Julie asked.

One of the nurses, having recognized Julie's voice, opened the curtain to usher us in. I thanked God, that's all I saw of Jason, was a thick gold chain, from which dangled, a small, melted pendant.

The team of doctors and nurses frantically worked on him. Julie and I just looked at one another. I pressed my lips shut to stop them from trembling, as we turned our attention to the young girl in the room.

Her thick, wavy brunette hair was pulled back, revealing her high cheekbones. Her large, deep blue eyes darted nervously, her face started to match the white shade of her blouse, as her expression changed rapidly from trembling and crying hysterically, to a state of shock. Thinking that she was on the verge of collapsing, Julie and I both took hold of an arm each, and led her to the relatives' room. She collapsed on the sofa, words tumbling out, faster and faster, until she ran out of breath.

We soon learnt from Lisa, his wife, that Jason was a part-time firefighter. He had been off duty, when a fire had started in a neighbour's house. Without hesitation, Jason had run inside to rescue the family. His burns were so severe that his own wife was unable to recognize him. I'm not sure that a firefighter's spouse could ever truly accept their loved one's job.

The sound of the door bursting open startled us all. A big, sturdy woman in her thirties with a no-nonsense attitude entered, followed by an older lady who appeared to be dressed for a special occasion.

I could tell that they had to be related. They all had the same blue eyes, high cheekbones and identical brunette hair, varying only in length. The conversation took an inevitable turn. For me, crying relatives were better than angry relatives, but the situation was still challenging.

"Who are you?" The older sister fixed Julie with a look of contempt. "What is happening? How is he? Someone had better start telling me, right now." Like a bird, she cocked her head, and inspected every detail of our appearance, from head to toe.

"My name is Julie, and this is Ros, we are here to offer any support we can for you and your family." Julie had perfected her show of empathy and her tone of voice for these situations, so as not to cause any offence. Not willing to address the sister again, she turned to the mother. "We will give you a moment with your daughter, while we go and see if we can get the doctor to speak to you."

Her mother walked over, to sit with her youngest daughter, I watched as she clasped the rosary beads tighter, in her hand. "Jason will be fine," she whispered. I felt a wave of relief, for I knew any kind of faith could only bring comfort to this family.

Moments before we reached the cubicle, to see if we could get an update, the alarms on the monitors sounded. Jason had gone into cardiac arrest and died.

The word was out, before I had even reached the waiting room. His fellow firefighters, heads in their hands, crying, were waiting to say their goodbyes to the man they saw as their brother. I could hear their thoughts, all in unison. A firefighter had to follow his own instincts, even if it meant disobeying a direct order. They all knew that every one of them would have run into that fire to save a life. I averted my eyes; watching grown men cry was deeply upsetting.

Over the course of the next few days, I questioned my spiritual job with Jason. Had I been invited in to help him cross, or had it just been a case of him wanting to share his experience? I tried to prevent my mind from reliving the upsetting events. I was still shaky from the experience, but the heaviness I'd felt earlier was slowly vanishing. Funny what a good cry can do.

I came to terms with the idea that I hadn't been meant to help pass Jason over to the Spirit World. I had convinced myself that he had passed himself over. But, a few days later, I had another vision:

I was standing in what reminded me of a large football field; however, there were no stands, no grass, no walls. Nothing but an empty space. Ten feet away, his back to me, stood Jason, his feelings currently lost in a fog of confusion, which filled my every thought. This poor man was trapped.

I was aware that if I walked up to him, I would startle the poor bloke (I was going to say, half to death, but perhaps that's not a good choice of words). I had to figure out a way of getting his attention without alarming him. As those very words crossed my mind, I looked around and saw a large red fire alarm, one that you would expect to see in a fire station. This one however, was suspended in thin air.

Although you would think that sounding off such a loud noise would certainly frighten the poor man, I knew differently. I hit the alarm and Jason snapped straight into working mode. Within seconds, like a true professional, he had dressed in about ninety pounds of gear and equipment, including a flame-resistant turnout coat, heavy steel-soled boots and a breathing pack.

I couldn't help but feel pride for the young man, as if he was my own son. Firefighters represent everything heroic and selfless to me.

He ran towards me for instructions, as though I was his duty officer. I didn't need to turn around to see the light of God's calling; I could feel it. Nothing that I have experienced on this earth could come close to the feeling; not even a mother's love could describe such an experience.

I turned and pointed to the tunnel of light, no words needed, but in my mind, it was as though the fire was on the other side, waiting for him. It was going so well, until he stopped abruptly.

"The heat, the heat, it's burning," Jason screamed. Despite his flameproof gear, he was overwhelmed. Flames shot up his legs and left side, then enveloped his chest. His whole six-foot-three, 210-pound frame was engulfed in fire. He ran toward me, before dropping on the floor, trying to roll and extinguish the flames.

My whole body shuddered involuntarily. The right side of my mouth, my ear and my nose felt charred and distorted. I couldn't breathe through my nose, and if I tried to breathe through my mouth, I could taste it; it didn't smell like burning, it had a fog of humanity to it. I knew it was human, and it was haunting. They say there is something about that smell that writes itself into your brain and cannot be erased.

Pure panic had set in, and I too was beginning to panic. Jason, screamed like a tortured animal, "HELP, HELP, PLEASE HEL…P!"

A thought burst into my consciousness. Without any hesitation, I yelled back, "The water! Run to the water! Run, run to the water!" The bright tunnel of light was now a breathtaking, beautiful, cascading waterfall.

Jason passed successfully, three days after his death

God bless, love and light Jason

Handbook Notes

This was the most graphic and tragic vision I have had, by far. The guilt I carry, as to whether I could have done anything differently to prevent him from reliving his death, still haunts me. So, what positives or learning can I take from Jason?

Jason came through a good week before, with information regarding his wife, sister, mother and fellow firefighters. The need to tell his story was important to him. It also proves that, in his last moments of life, he was able to leave his body and witness everyone else's reactions. I do find comfort in that thought.

It was the hardest case to write up, as normally I go straight into the full vision, but with Jason that didn't happen until three days after his death.

All my crossings have been set in different scenes, very few have been as you or I would expect, that being a beam of light entering the room and they rise to it.

I have spoken about God's calling and how the light is not only full of love, but warms your very soul. This feeling of warmth had triggered Jason back to reality, to the moment and circumstance of his death in a fire.

I hate to think that it was a cruel lesson on Jason's part, that I had to learn, I could use the light in many different forms, such as the waterfall. It seems a lesson learnt, at Jason's expense and it greatly troubles me. However, as I have said about Grace's lesson," I should be we," and I must trust my Guides.

"Many can offer a hand to guide, but only those that choose to, can lead the darkness into the light. Walk with us and ask not of us, to be by your side, but to follow you with protection and love. Free will, will be given to you only, hence your task and not ours. Trust we are with you and never allow your doubts, or others to destroy that. Negativity feeds your mind, not your soul. You are human, my child, and we understand restrictions, but we would not ask for your help, if your soul had not chosen this.

Your path is not divided, but branches off, as you have an ability to spread the workload. Followers will flock, and with their commitment, you will together rescue the suffering, and by doing so witness a new light enter your plane. A great deal of work is being put in place here as we speak. Our plight is being answered by those that listen and new guides will bring forward those lost into your circles.

Never look back, my love, we are there.

—Monk

CHAPTER 9: VOLUNTEERING

I am very lucky to be self-employed, to have a paid job that allows me the free time to do both volunteer work and to spend time with my spiritual learning. I have been asked a few times why I do voluntary work. My answer is, because I can. I know of many people who would love to offer their services, but simply don't have the time.

When my sister-in-law passed, I had been going to the Spiritualist Church for a few months, and was following my path of healing, as that was what it was at the time. Don't even get me started on healing, I could write a whole new book on the problems I had with that, but on the plus side, healing cured my Crohn's disease.

It was at this time that I met Terry, an older man at the church, who often had very little to say, but when he did, it was wise. He had been involved in a new project at the hospice, called Death Talk. Although the name sounds cold and shocking, he invited me to go along and see what I thought about it.

Once at Death Talk, I shared my experience regarding my sister-in-law, and found it refreshing to be able to talk openly about it. How it was such a rewarding experience, to be able to help both my family and sister-in-law. Without knowing it beforehand, I had found something that I desperately wanted to do. One lady commented, "You would be a re-birthing partner."

From that one meeting, the doors opened quickly. I was invited to volunteer in the day unit at the hospice once a week, and also to take part in a new project within the hospital, to assist in the Palliative Care Unit, offering an end of life bedside vigil service for the terminally ill.

I would like to explain my volunteering job a little more. I work as part of a team within the Palliative Care Unit. End of life palliative care is for people diagnosed with any terminal illness, where a cure is not possible. The aim is to treat or manage pain and any other physical symptoms, presenting themselves at the end of life. It also helps any psychological, social or spiritual needs. It is important to point out that the end of life Palliative

Care Team helps patients to live as well as possible until they actually die, and to die with dignity.

The team providing this help ask patients about their wishes and preferences, to form a plan of care. This is a holistic approach, because it deals with each individual as a "whole" person.

When studying the feedback from these terminal patients, it was apparent that their greatest fear was not to be left alone during their final hours. This was the reason for the setting up of the vigil team service, offering comfort and companionship to them.

Although some refer to us as a soul midwife within the hospital, I have since learnt that there is an organization out there, under the same name. I must stress I am in no way connected to them. I thought about changing my title to numerous things, re-birthing partner, twilight service, light-worker, but soul midwife is the name given to us by the nurses on duty.

Sitting vigil, or assisting someone in death, as I mentioned before carried two meanings. From the hospital's and patient's point of view, I am simply just a reassuring hand to hold. From my point of view, this is no walk in the park. I see two major concerns, my intellectual human side is well aware that this at times is going to be hard and upsetting. I know that, due to the patients' conditions, these are not going to be all peaceful experiences. I could be wrong: maybe, as I have been chosen to assist with the help of my guides (Doc and Monk), I can help to make this happen.

My other concern is that spirituality regarding crossing overs, was not accepted, or addressed, in the hospital or hospice. I knew from the moment I offered to volunteer with the vigil service (and had been screened for any conflicts of interests that would put patient safety at risk), I needed to keep my religion and beliefs totally secret.

However, what about, the spirit, the soul? Yes, the hospital had a Chaplain on duty, and that was wonderful for those patients that had a belief in God, but for those with no religious beliefs, lost or otherwise, they were the ones at risk. I am assuming that if we are called upon, it is because they didn't want a Chaplain. I presume this means that they have no faith. My question is, would they go to the light, when they depart? If they didn't, perhaps through fear or not wanting to leave the earthly plane, they would be left trapped. One trapped soul is one too many.

I cannot underestimate the spiritual work I need to put into both protecting myself and the terminally ill patients whom I am sitting with. This reminds me of the lady with the death rattle. Luckily she didn't attach herself to me, however, I am well aware that this can happen, and has done so.

Regarding my spiritual vigils, and this is what my book is based on. If you are reading this book, both you and I know that there is absolutely no difference between a soul with a physical body and one without. In truth, this book goes on to explain just how important it is that these trapped souls find help.

I have now learnt never to underestimate the Intelligence of our guides. They know, before you or I will ever know, what things must be done, shown or given in ways that fit our individual purpose, and why. Despite continuing to go to development classes, my fear of connecting with spirit grew stronger. I longed for the love and light that was talked about when connecting. The vibrations I picked up felt uncomfortable even threatening at times. It was repeated that we attract like for like within the church, so I had to keep my fears and feelings to myself. This hindered my development, and made me worried as to what torment or evil I might hold within me that made me attract such spirits. I withdrew from any form of connection bar that of my guides.

Whilst in one of the development classes, we were asked to ask our guides for either an object or words to show us where our future spiritual path would lie. Although I didn't understand the meaning of mine straight away, I was shown a hospital ward. Four unoccupied beds lined either side of the room. Seconds later, I was a judge, gavel in hand. The emotions I felt overwhelmed me, as the responsibility of not judging was immense.

It wasn't long after this vision that my work as a spiritual rescue medium started, and the reason as to why this was centered around a ward became clear. By showing me a person in bed, in need, in physical form although obviously in a vision, I had no fear, my compassion allowing me to connect through my heartstrings, as I did with my sister-in-law and my physical job. It was an ingenious way to help, which made me embrace these lost spirits without even realising I was working with the dead.

I talked about finding commonalities and patterns. These commonalities range from many emotional issues, and may cloud the moment the light appears to aid these souls into the afterlife. I have tried to choose the cases that involve a variety of issues, such as lack of faith, fear of judgement or earthly attachments, to name but a few. Also, I would like to confirm that none of the cases in this book were taken from experiences in the hospice.

The patterns come from the way they come through. From experience, this is very different from anything I have experienced in development class. As a medium, I find them only too willing and eager to talk to me, by whatever senses that may be.

When a trapped spirit comes through, they seem almost as confused as I am, as to why they are here. I have never had a trapped spirit talk openly to me. The first thing that I pick up on is their emotional issues, in the vibrations they give off. This is something that is very frightening and uncomfortable. Sometimes, over a course of a few days or weeks, I slowly get to see parts of their life or issues. Once I start to feel braver, the connection lasts longer and longer, until the time comes that my Guides know that we are both ready to blend.

The reason as to why they didn't pass creates a visual energy, an imprint, locked in this negative circle. I personally don't know if they live this day in or day out, since their death. I don't think so. What I believe is when they are ready to try to transition again, it is only with the help of a Rescue Medium that they are able to break this cycle. I become a part of their imprint, living and playing a vital part in their dreams or nightmares.

CHAPTER 10: DANNY

As I sat in my office, shuffling paperwork, my senses quickly picked up spirit around me. Unable to dismiss it, I sat quietly and allowed everything around me to quickly dissolve. Images of what looked like a war zone started to materialize. Half of me knew that I had been thrust into a very alien world, about to start a battle, except somehow I looked and felt like an animated cartoon. The other half of me felt that I was a spectator looking at myself within the computer screen, about to play a game.

Within minutes, all hell was let loose. people were running about, shooting their guns and throwing hand grenades. I just stood there, not having a clue as to what I was doing or what I had to do. I felt my faithful Monk and Doc (my spirit guides) by my side.

"What am I supposed to do?" I asked.

"You need to rescue the named boy, Danny." Monk pointed to the young man in the distance, who had a red sniper's silhouette around him.

"How am I supposed to do that? I'm not shooting anyone," I said, trying to shake off the sniper gun, glued to my hand. "Will I die if I get shot?"

"Ros, this is as alien to us as it is to you, but we will try to help."

By now, Danny was so far out of sight that I started running down the deserted street. Running, in this instance, is not the correct word. I was bobbing along, which did put a smile on my face. Bang! I felt something hit me. I, being the spectator, was unhurt, however a glimpse at the screen showed my health level declining. I had just been shot, yet unhurt, I continued to run.

It all suddenly became clear. I have walked into my son's bedroom plenty of times whilst he was playing computer games. I realised now that I was taking part in a reality game and the health bar wasn't looking too good. Okay, so now I understood what It was that I needed to do and where I was. *Two can play at this game*, I said to myself as I hid behind a parked car, planning my strategy.

All I needed to do was avoid snipers and catch up with Danny. *It can't be too hard*, I thought: famous last words, as ammunition came raining down on me and I found myself back at base, at the start.

"Right Doc, Monk, you need to be my lookouts. I need to avoid snipers. Are you ready?"

This time, instead of walking down the middle of the street, I started playing the game, hugging buildings and hiding in doorways, as both my guides pointed out the danger. Occasionally, I would get the other half of me to pull up the game statistics, showing my health record and Danny's whereabouts on the map. It wasn't long, despite our best efforts, that we were sent back to base, each time allowing Danny to be further out of reach.

Although we were getting further into the game each time, I knew I was such a novice in the mind field, that I began to lose my patience. This time, instead of running and hiding, I decided to try to reason with the other players. Perhaps I could convince them to help protect me, and help me to reach Danny. Ignoring my sense of imminent doom, I bravely walked into the middle of the road.

"Guys, I need your help, I need to….."

Bang, bang, bang, bang, I heard and found myself back at the base.

"Well, that didn't work," laughed Doc.

"I can't do this. I don't know what to do, and if one more little bleep thinks it's funny to shoot a woman, I will scream. This is literally above and beyond the call of duty." I grimaced, not willing to share the irony with my guides.

There was a rapid change from optimism to pessimism, followed by frustration as we began to lose all hope of ever catching up with him.

"Let's think about this," I said. "I recall something about health portions, being hidden so they can be used to get us further. There is also a game in which you can actually drive tanks, so let's see if we can do this." Feeling revved up, like an engine, off we went.

After what felt like hours of play, we managed to get closer to Danny; so close, in fact, that I no longer needed to pull the map up, I could see the red silhouette about ten feet away.

"Danny," I shouted.

Danny stopped and turned round. His eyes had a look of those of a dog, ready to fight over its territory, as he opened fire. It honestly hadn't occurred to me that he would shoot me.

Back at base, I was all but done in. This constant effort became unbearable, my emotions were bouncing between frustration, despair, and anger. The feeling of anger was not something I was used to in my life; somehow it didn't seem appropriate in a rescue. I was so wrapped up in the game, I had reached my boiling point. Doc and Monk looked at me with the same defeated expression.

I had to think logically. I needed to get a grip on reality. The reality was my keyword, as the spectator part of me, sat at the computer desk, bent down and pulled the plug out of the socket disconnecting the game. Suddenly, it all changed, there we were standing in a field, with nothing but green grass and a hilltop, there was no war zone in sight.

"What the bleep did you do that for? Loser! Just because I shot you. You shouldn't be playing games anyway." He went on and on. I listened, as the words tumbled out, like verbal bullets.

Standing in front of me was Danny, a young boy of around fourteen or fifteen years old. Five foot nothing. His Adam's apple bobbed furiously, as his words fell on deaf ears. He reminded me of a younger version of my own son, with his mannerisms and the way he talked, but my son swore less (I hope). His pale face, just a shade darker than albino, highlighted his cute freckles. His lean body was dressed in a combat cotton shirt and jeans.

I waited until his voice became quieter and he was becoming less animated. Despite the venomous look on his face and his mouthy attitude, I found him entertaining, rather than offensive.

It took several minutes for him to calm down. In the meantime, ignoring his remarks, I prepared myself, needing to put on my Mother's commanding voice, one that was hidden behind a veil, as he had gone too far this time. Instead, like a big softie, I spoke gently.

"Danny, my name is Ros and I have been sent here to…"

I broke off, as we both became aware of the sound of music coming from over the hill, in our new surroundings. An eagle circled against the beautiful blue sky, dotted with what looked like candy floss fluffy clouds, beckoning us to go closer.

Danny's mood changed immediately as we both smiled and ran up the hill. The music grew louder as we saw in full view, the massive structures of a funfair. The big wheel stood proudly in its bright colours. Loud hysterical screams could be heard from the top of the rollercoaster.

"Race you to the dodgems," shouted an excited Danny, as he ran off to explore the funfair.

"No bumping and no crashing," shouted the ticket man with his cheeky grin and a wink, as he took us to our cars.

"Hope you drive better than you shoot," smirked Danny.

"I wouldn't be so cocky now, little one, you're on my level now," I shouted as I headed directly for him. Playful revenge was sweet.

For the next two hours, Danny dragged me from one ride to another, until my body could stand no more of the whirling, twirling and spinning. My voice-box needed a rest from all the hysterical screaming.

"Hungry?" I gasped, begging for a rest.

"I'm starving," he replied.

Standing outside the food van, I read aloud the menu, "Burger, chips, hot dogs, nachos, popcorn, ice-cream, candy floss?"

"Yes, please," he replied, laughing, I obliged and ordered everything.

Laughing and exhausted, we sat down on the warm grass, tucking into our feast. It was good to see Danny eating and enjoying himself. My instincts told me it was overdue and that he had been poorly for a long time, missing out on the life we know and take for granted.

We both shut our eyes for a minute as the music softened, to respect our need for a little peace. In the distance, I could hear a pinging sound from a shooting tin can game.

"Would you rather have a bullet to the head, or two to the chest and bleed to death?" Danny asked. He had a serious look on his face, but he could have been pulling my leg.

Well, that was not a question I was expecting, "Really, Danny, you're not still thinking about that silly game again are you?"

There was no answer. I sensed that he was waiting for my response.

"One to the head, of course," I replied a little too quickly, but suddenly as the words left my tongue, I was catapulted back in my mind, to being sat at the train station with Grace. I was reminded of how I felt when I thought I was dead and how I would have done anything to have gone back, even if it was just for a day, to say my goodbyes. I considered the implications of what he had just asked.

"Actually, Danny, I will take that back and have two to the chest instead."

He didn't say anything, and I didn't need to comment on why he had asked such a loaded question. It was clear to me that he had put up a good fight for the sake of others and by doing so, he also had taken bullets to the chest, in fact, a lot more than two. I reached my hand over to touch his, I could feel the wetness of the tears in my eyes.

"Stop it, weirdo," he whispered, as he continued to eat and fill his seemingly hollow legs. I felt so proud of this brave young man.

Slowly but softly, I felt a change in the atmosphere, a small electrical pulse seemed to be getting closer.

A young, strikingly beautiful girl, with long brunette hair, was walking in our direction, her energy gravitating towards Danny, and vice versa.

"Close your mouth, you're not a fish, Danny," I teased, as she walked closer. Her eyes locked onto the food, trying to hide her embarrassment.

"Hello sweets, are you here alone?" I said.

"Yes, I think so, I can't find my friends."

"Would you like to join us, we have far too much food. That's okay with you, isn't it, Danny?"

"Whatever," he said, an octave too high. His verbal skills were very limited all of a sudden.

"My name's Ros and this is Danny. You're welcome to join us for the day. In fact, I would be grateful for an excuse not to go on another ride."

"Amy, thank you. I'm Amy, I mean," the poor sweet girl was becoming increasingly tongue-tied.

Danny's eyes glued to her every movement was generating an intense spark. He smiled a nervous, manly, "Alright."

Once we had eaten, we headed for the house of mirrors. There was nothing like breaking the ice than a good laugh at our own distorted reflection. The man with the nice smile, who was now on the Waltzers, shouted over to us.

"The louder you scream, the faster you go," he said, holding open the car door, giving me yet another of his winks.

We continued for hours, indulging in the magic of the day. Like a lioness now protecting her young, I watched as they grew closer and I was able to hang back in the hustle and bustle of the crowds.

In a short span of time, whilst they were talking, it was obvious to see they had grown very fond of each other. The noise of the funfair became silent, as a voice over the tannoy announced that the rides were closing.

My initial exhilaration soon wore off, and my spirit started to sink, as I realized the day was coming to an end. I wanted to rewind, go back and replay the scenes over and over, again and again.

Danny and Amy, both now holding hands, ran towards another ride, before stopping and turning to me.

"Ros, did you want to come on this ride?" Danny looked down at the last two tickets he held in his hand.

"That's okay," I said, smiling at him with pride and admiration. Now was not the time to let my emotions get in the way.

Amy threw her arms around me and kissed my cheek. "Thank you for a lovely day and for introducing me to your son."

"You're welcome, sweets, but he's not my…" Suddenly, I didn't want to correct her. I would have been proud to have him as my son. "Look after each other, won't you?" I knew this was going to be the last time I would see them.

Danny had no words for me and merely stared back at me with wetness in his eyes. Shy or not, street cred or no street cred, there was no way I was going to let him get away without a cuddle. "Bye." That was all my voice-box would let out.

"Bye, Ros. Thank you."

I watched as the ticket man escorted them to the carriage. I felt a strange stirring of recognition. I had met this man before, but couldn't quite place him. As they entered the archway, the bright lights above twinkled. It was the 'Tunnel of Light.'

"Good job," winked the gatekeeper.

God bless, love and light, Danny and Amy

Handbook Notes

Sweet, sweet Danny; I will never forget my time with him. He brings tears of pride to my eyes, just saying his name. So what was the lesson with Danny?

A few days after Danny, I was at work in the hospice, when I saw a lady sitting in the garden, tissues in hand. I approached her with a smile and asked if she would like some company, to which she shrugged; a cue to sit with her. We gently talked about the weather, until she felt confident enough to tell me that her husband was in the ward and she had been called in. She had sat with him all night and had to just get some fresh air. She cried, bless her, and wished that he would just pass, as it was cruel to keep him alive, suffering and in pain.

We talked a little about the law and how we wouldn't let our animals suffer. At that moment, her daughter joined us and I was left with her parting question, "How can there be a God that allows such suffering?"

Danny's question to me, if you remember, was, " Would I take a bullet to the head, or two to the chest?" This taught me so much. It was clear that Danny chose to suffer, to stay with his loved ones on this earth. He seemed to have the option to die, by taking the one bullet to end his suffering, but it was the bravest, most selfless thing one can do, to remain as long as one can with their loved ones on this earth.

I wish I had had the knowledge at the time to try to explain gently to the lady in the garden that the strength of her husband's suffering was, in fact, the strength of his love for her. I would have hoped that she could have changed the negative feelings of pain and suffering in his last days to an appreciation of the measurement of love for her, a testament to his strength.

My lesson from this was to try not to feel sympathy for patients hanging on and suffering, but to admire them for their bravery in holding on.

This was confirmed again in mid-December, as I sat with a 95-year-old gentleman, during his last hours. His first and only words to me were, "How long is it till Christmas?"

CHAPTER 11: DEVELOPMENT CLASS

*I*n 2016, I dedicated my life to God, for Him to guide me on whatever journey He saw fit. I wanted, more than anything, to understand the whole purpose of our being here, what it was all about spiritually, and more importantly to understand my purpose on this earth.

I decided to join the local Spiritualist Church. This is my diary post. All my diary posts and guidance shared happened over a period of roughly one year, before I started both my volunteering job and rescue work. I believe this was the training I needed to gently ease me in.

Diary Entry 11th March 2016

A few nights ago I went to a development group at the local spiritualist church for the first time in 20 years. I had an enjoyable evening with lovely people. Nothing enlightening happened that night, but I felt comfortable to be in a safe environment, to start to learn more.

All that changed the next day. I was excited and decided I would try meditation for the first time, to see what I would feel. Oh boy, did I regret that. Images rushed through me and stayed with me for three whole days, on constant replay, nothing I could do could either stop it or alter it in any way. I was at breaking point by day three.

I had to go back to the church for help, but sadly didn't get any.

My vision took me back to the development group. There were thirteen of us sat in a circle, five of them were men. I have the song, "Bridge over troubled water," by Simon and Garfunkel, constantly repeating itself to me.

I felt like I was sitting in a very fast-moving car, and out of the window all this information was rushing by me, very quickly. I couldn't breathe or talk, not even to ask them to stop or slow down. When I could piece it together, this is what I observed. I saw one of the men in our group in deep, troubled black water, drowning in emotional waves. I saw a bridge over him, however, this bridge is a tangle of spirits (his loved ones' arms and legs, linked). They can't reach down and pull him out, as the bridge would collapse (I feel at this point he thought spirit had abandoned him).

Immediately after, I saw the present. He has now managed to drag himself out of the water and he has both hands on the bridge, together with one foot.

Suddenly, my vision changes, I am back in school, standing in the science block. I see five small boxes in front of me. These five boxes were used to make a bridge arch: by supporting each other's weight, the bridge was strong, but if one box was taken away, the bridge collapsed.

I would like to ask this man whether he knew of someone who had passed with ill feelings. If he did, it would be really important to know that this spirit person was now completing the bridge and without him or her, it would not be properly supported. (The man in the group must take this as a peace sign, I feel strongly about this). It will lighten his load.

On the other side, I can see the sun's rays reach the halfway point on the bridge. I am now standing at the halfway mark; the sun hitting me warms me, like nothing I have felt before. I am bathing in what I can only imagine is God's love. Once the man in our group makes it to the halfway mark and he steps into the light, I feel this will end his pain. (LOVELY FEELING)

End of post.

When I wrote this in my diary, I woke up the next day feeling balanced. Everything in the house looked sharper and brighter, as though I had just been given new prescription glasses to try on. I had not been aware of a change. I could pull up the images of the vision, without it playing from start to finish. Now that I could think clearly, I thought about the man whom the message was for, only to realize that there was no fifth man in that circle. I could see him clearly in my mind, yet he was not in the circle that night. Although this experience blew my mind, the critic in me started questioning if I had suddenly developed an overactive imagination. Fast forward three months, I had started going to another church, it was here that I met Terry, who helped me accept and understand my visions.

Diary Entry 22nd June 2016
Today, Terry came round for a chat. We talked a little about last night, (at the development group). I found the courage to tell him about my bridge over troubled water experience, from three months ago. He jumped for joy, pacing my kitchen and asked if I had looked back at the man on the bridge to see if he was still there? I hadn't. He went on to explain that I had done my first assisted crossing over and was thrilled for me. I was absolutely shocked, I had no idea such things happened.

I continued going to the development classes and experienced the spiritual highs connecting with my guides, but it was clear that I wasn't going down the traditional path of mediumship. Below is another example.

End of post.

Diary Entry 3rd August 2016

Yesterday's class concentrated on healing, I was looking forward to it all through the week, hoping that maybe something would fall into place, and it would take me down the path that I wished to go. Well, it sure took me down something.

Before I went to the church, both Terry and I had gone to death chat in the hospice. On leaving, we headed for the church.

Unable to find a parking space, we were late arriving. Once through the door, I could hear them upstairs. They seemed much louder than normal, and instantly I was overcome by an uneasy feeling. As I walked into the room, I saw that the tutor, Peter, was absent. I sat there for a few minutes, then I had to leave the room. What was wrong with me? I just wasn't feeling well. The energy was all wrong and I felt pain shooting down my left hand side of my body.

Peter arrived, and the class began. We didn't start with healing, which was such a shame. Instead, we meditated.

I became aware that I could see myself sitting in a chair, with my hands handcuffed behind me and the key was in my mouth. The only thing that could free me, was to talk.

Peter asked me if I could explain it. I declined; my pain was getting too intense. Towards the end of the night, I felt so bad that I had no choice but to ask for help.

I was certain that if the pain wasn't physically mine, it had to be coming from someone within the circle, but no one could claim it.

Then, it suddenly dawned on me that I had walked through the hospice ward, and wondered if I had possibly picked up this pain from there? Both Terry and Peter instantly agreed. Katie asked if she could channel some healing, in fact the whole group sent healing, compounding the energy. It was lovely and it did help, for by the time I drove home, the pain had left me.

End of post

Diary Entry 4th August 2016

I spoke with Terry today, who explained more about the fact that I had picked up a spirit from the ward, and how sometimes, they need an escape, or find a way out of their pain, perhaps that is what had happened. I had forgotten about spiritual pain, and the possibility of them attaching themselves to you. He added that he thought Eve, my Guide, had done such a good job holding off the pain, until I arrived at the church, where help could be given.

Today I feel a lot better, he asked if I had got anywhere with Eve? But sadly, I have to say no, A thought crossed my mind this afternoon and I am slightly worried about it, when I was sitting on a chair with my hands tied and the key in my mouth, it occurred to me that maybe Eve is telling me I can't or shouldn't be doing hands-on healing. I hope this isn't the case, I certainly don't wish to become a medium!

End of post

Diary Entry 9th August 2016

Earlier in the week, I was given a task by spirit, to carry out at the next group meeting.

I need to backtrack here as I haven't been very good at keeping up with my diary. I talked about picking up the pain on my left side on Tuesday evening. This continued to get worse over the next few days. I decided to go and lie down on my bed and ask for healing from Eve.

Next minute, I had drifted off and when I awoke, I had a clear understanding that the pain belonged to a biker in his early twenties. I couldn't or didn't communicate with him, but had the vision of sliding down the road, on my left-hand side.

I knew that I had to learn to understand this. It was a task, another learning exercise, I needed Roger, the quiet person in the group, interested in soul rescues, to be a part of it.

I spoke at great length with Terry about it, he accepted all this, as it had been given by Eve, my guide and was to be trusted.

I am worried, maybe I am an open vessel, for all to come through, how long was the queue of spirits. Where would it lead? I wouldn't be worried if it wasn't for the pain that I had experienced.

I was also concerned about this upcoming task. As Roger and I were both beginners, there was a danger that we could do more harm than good. He assured me that making no preconditions nor presumptions, with our Guides' help, no harm could be done.

He later spoke to Peter (the tutor), to quite rightly ask permission, as he had a responsibility for us all. Peter agreed that it was alright to do what was needed, but wanted a quick chat with me first.

End of post

Diary Entry 11th August 2016

Got to the church tonight feeling very anxious. Peter asked for a private word. He talked about forgetting everything I had ever done or learnt, and to just put it down to experience. He also said that Joules was under-qualified to have given me what he had, and that Eve was the only one to be trusted.

He then went on to talk about how he had used his gift to go round giving private readings and had learnt that it was wrong. He talked again about materialistic things and how they needed to be stripped back.

Needless to say, the task did not happen. Where I go with it, I don't know.

I forgot to say that when I briefly explained the pain that I get is too much. He replied that he could stop it all now, to which I freaked, and declined. I didn't want it to be completely taken away, I knew when I said that, he had misunderstood again. I knew if he took the pain sensation away, I could no longer help anyone and no longer feel the need to help take away someone's pain. I meant it from my heart. Given the choice, I would choose this pain to relieve others, no matter how intense it is.

At the close of class, Peter asked me to open for healing, but I declined. I was so hurt that he could judge Joules. Going back to the task, I am really aware of bikers on the road tonight behind me, not one but three. I hope I haven't failed Eve in my task and that the biker is looked after and taken over to the spirit world.

Wednesday 1.11am

Just woke up from a message from Eve as follows:

"My petal, firstly thank you for looking for the rose, you remember well. You are a good student and yes, full circle is where you are going. Do you recall the very first time at this church, what do you know now that you could have learnt on that night? You have felt it and known this, but your kindness stops your judgment when a good heart is present. Maybe that is something to learn from.

Going back to the first night we sent you to that church, Peter was meant to give you a reading from your flower. We stripped you of your beauty, all that was left was a stem. Although beautiful and purposeful in its own right, we chose for you not to have a reading, for no one can judge you or see your beauty correctly.

Remember the lesson given to you by Joules, about attachments.

Your innocence in the way you talk about being a beginner is commendable, but somewhat misleading to others, however, we respect your free will and your humbleness in portraying this.

This church allowed you to find your voice, but like I have shown you, your words can be misunderstood. I feel your pain of the echoing of the word, patience. Some see it as a weakness, we see it as one of your strengths. Seek and you will find. Your thoughts are manifesting into form. Focus on your desires and not upon your fears.

—Eve

I asked her about the biker, but she didn't reply. Instead, the biker stepped forward and kissed me on my forehead. This was encouraging for me.

End of post

The following week was my last time in that church. Once we got there, Peter, the tutor was absent. Instead, the class was taken by two of the committee members, who informed us at the end of the evening that this was the last development class, as Peter was no longer coming back.

CHAPTER 12: NYAH

As any parent would know, when your child stands over you and wakes you up in the middle of the night after having a bad dream, your natural half-asleep instinct is to lift the covers up and invite them in. This was my reaction when Nyah did just that.

The only difference was, I have no daughter, and Nyah was of spirit form. As she lay next to me, sniffling, I snuggled up close to offer comfort. In a flash, Nyah's tragic life became clear.

She was the eldest of three, from a small village somewhere in India. Her brother, four years her junior, and her sister, aged six, were her life. Her parents would give them everything they could afford, and thankfully, love was free.

Nyah and her brother would play for hours. She dreamed of being a teacher one day, and wanted to set up a special school for her younger sister, who had learning disabilities. Her brother dreamed of being a builder, and would sit and plan the design of the school for her to teach in.

As puberty grew near, Nyah started to attract unwanted male attention. This was of great concern for the family. It was agreed that a 'Bride Price' would be put upon her head, despite having only just reached her teens. The price was met by a city man, at least three times her age. He promised not only to look after Nyah, but would also support the family.

She was fourteen years old when she married, and the life she had quickly changed. Now living in the city, she was put to work cleaning. When she wasn't working, she was locked in a room and half-starved. All hopes of teaching and the school her brother would build were slowly being erased from her dreams.

My heart broke as I witnessed the true events of a violation of human rights that robbed Nyah of her childhood, subjecting a fourteen-year-old to a life of violence and abuse. The consequences of this marriage were catastrophic. Nyah fell pregnant, but sadly, without any medical aid, suffered an ectopic pregnancy and died.

Thank God, it was seconds before Doc and Monk stepped in, and play time began.

In front of us both was the most intricate eighteenth-century doll's house I have ever seen. Twenty-four lavish rooms in total, complete with marble and french-polished floors. Stunning tapestries lined the walls in the grand dining room, while soft furnishings graced the bedrooms. It was nothing short of an incredible, precise, miniature masterpiece. Delicate tiny electrical wall lights and a crystal chandelier highlighted the whimsical winding staircase, fit for a queen.

Nyah's face lit up, and we played for hours. No longer did I feel or see myself as an adult entertaining a child. I too was transported back to being a kid, as we allowed our imaginations to run free within this fantasy world, acting out the most enchanting stories.

The bathrooms were one of Nyah's favorite rooms. Roll-top porcelain baths, with hand-painted fine flowers complemented the gilded twenty-four carat gold leaf taps, complete with running water. There were even flushing toilets. But the room she loved the most was the library. Books lined the walls, scaled down to no bigger than one's smallest finger nail.

It was Nyah's wish fulfillment, and a joy to see this fourteen-year-old playing house, rather than having to clean a house. A bittersweet feeling suddenly came over me as a realisation of what I was there for crept in. The thought crossed my mind that I wanted her to feel like a princess, if only for one day. I was confused as to why such a lovely vision would have a bitter edge to it.

The sound of dancing hooves came closer. We turned to see two elegant dapple grey horses, with such poise and grace, heading our way. Their plumed feathers, manes and tails blew softly in the breeze. They pulled the most exquisite white carriage, decorated with beautiful pink and white floral garlands.

Two uniformed coaching staff beamed with glee; of course these were Doc and Monk.

The bittersweet feeling was now overwhelming, as I lay back in my bed alone.

God bless, love and light, Nyah.

Handbook Notes

Crossing over children can be very upsetting. Thanks to my guides I was shown that although I had to see the circumstances of her death, we have the ability to make dreams come true. Another example of a child's crossing happened in the rescue circle up north. They had a very young boy that they struggled with. He loved trains and counting. Five of them spent over twenty minutes, trying to get him to jump on the train on the count of three.

Nyah, like all the others, will never leave my heart. And in loving memory of her, and her dream to teach, I now sponsor a wonderful African children's charity, which invests 100% of your donation into education and care.

CHAPTER 13: ASTRAL PLANES

My husband and I have been lucky enough to travel to some beautiful places in this world, more so now that my boys are young adults, yet no matter how lovely these were, by the end of the second week, despite being able to keep in contact, I would start pining.

So I had a great fear of dying and not being able to play a physical part in my family's life. Having faith, and knowing I was only able to watch from a distance really did cause me anxiety. Nothing was going to convince me otherwise, this was going to be my hell. My rational brain hoped that spirit would have the ability to either rip my heart out or wipe my memory clean, yet neither of these would make sense, spiritually.

Continuing with my personal development with Joules, I questioned the above.

Vision

I was shown an elderly man sitting in his lounge, reading his newspaper. He sat in his favourite chair, surrounded by his belongings. On the mantelpiece, I could see family pictures and a clock. The time was just after 1pm. This man was totally at peace, waiting for his wife to get in from work. At 5pm, his wife walked through the door.

He turned to his wife to greet her and asked, "What's for dinner?"

Cheeky thing! I must admit I felt his greeting should have been, "Hello love, dinner will be ready in five minutes."

That was it, my vision over.

I was sitting in my kitchen, with a cup of coffee in my hand. I looked up to see the oven, the clock read 13.13. I wasn't quite sure what to take from this vision, until the thought crossed my mind, did he actually know that he had passed?

Suddenly, my mind went into overdrive as I looked back at the time. What if Joules appeared and told me I too was dead, and had been for the last year.

Have I created my heaven, sat in my kitchen, waiting for my husband and boys to come home? What if I had been dead for years like the man in my vision and was not aware of it?

A peace came over me, as I knew for sure that my husband was going to be home from work just after 5pm today, shortly followed by my boys. So if I was dead, it was impossible for me to feel grief. I didn't even have to wait two weeks, two years or twenty years. However long it was going to be I could feel no grief, knowing I would see them in a few hours, witnessing the fact that time had no meaning.

That simple vision ended all my fears.

I will share with you now, a few more simple visions shown to me over a period of time. I want you to visualize a man at sea with his faithful dog, the calm waters and sunshine soothing his soul, simply feeling fulfilled by the love he shares with his dog and the sea. Allow yourselves to feel his peace and tranquility.

Next, I want you to visualize a man who loves nothing more than counting his money. This man sits in a bank vault, floor to ceiling with gold. Again, I want you to feel his contentment he receives from creating his surroundings.

I will continue to claim I am not a working medium, not being able to connect with one's loved ones and give messages. But on a couple of occasions, something has slipped through. On both occasions, they were three-day events and troubled me.

One of these very important messages came through, I was unaware at the time that it was the previous minister of the church. In the message, she talked about how she continued to work within the church, that she had helped to create. This was her place of Heaven on Earth when she was alive, and now passed, she continued to work in her church, creating a piece of Earth in Heaven.

Once again, visualize this scene, feel her love within her church. This was the final image I needed to validate and join the above scenes together.

Now I want you to see a street in Heaven; walk down that street and look at your neighbours. The man sat at home waiting for his wife, the man at sea with his dog, the man in his bank vault and at the end of this street, the church. These people, apart from the minister, of course, were totally unaware that they had passed.

Like my own thoughts, supposing this very second you have the realization that you have passed. Where you sit or lie now, reading this book, is what you have created. You are waiting for your loved ones to visit or come home. How does it make you feel? How long have you been like this? How long before you see your loved ones, today, tomorrow, at the weekend? When was the last time you saw or spoke to them? This morning, yesterday? I bet it wasn't years ago. If this was true, does grief exist for you right now? Having seen the visual proof of the above, especially the man in his lounge gives me the peace I needed.

This may be the concept and the meaning, when mediums refer to, there being no time in the spirit world.

So what does heaven look like? On first thoughts, I can't help thinking of the old cliché: pearly gates, white clouds, people floating around in white gowns. Picturing all these scenes above, is heaven simply full of streets made up of anything we simply wish it to be?

So what does heaven feel like? As I walk from one neighbour to another, I notice that they all have the same feeling. I was shocked at this, as I would have expected to feel seasick at sea, and at the bank vault, uninspired and bored. Yet each one felt heavenly.

It got me thinking. I live in a small seaside village. If I were to visit anywhere in the world, I might say things like, "It reminds me of the village," or, "It smells like the village," but I would never say, "It feels like my village." The only time I can recall saying something felt like Heaven would be in that moment of pure relaxation.

Have you ever said, "This feels just like Jupiter."? No. How could we possibly know what that feels like?

So, is this a recall from our souls? I do believe we are reborn many times and deep down we all have knowledge and feelings that we must try to tap into.

Don't forget that I am not claiming this to be the only true answer, or right for you. Joules taught me, wisdom is a deeper state of understanding.

These images sit with me, more than a glove; more like an inner skin. Maybe we are all shown different things, answers that they know will fit our needs. What I love so much about these visions is the simplicity of them all, how one image speaks volumes to me. These are not in any order and not always relevant to the crossings over, but they are too valuable in my eyes to keep to myself. They also support and validate for me the bigger picture in a future chapter.

A few weeks later, I had another vision, one that continued and took me a step higher than above. This time, I was with Guyirl, my guardian, looking down on the street. There was a reason behind this. I asked a question, after a conversation with my mother.

"If a man had committed sin, surely, he could not go to heaven and have his mansion, and all his money that his heart desired?"

Guyirl responded,

"We are not capable of denying man or woman of anything that they desire, by not allowing them this would be to judge, and it is not spiritually possible for us to judge. You must understand that we do not live in our bodies or minds, we are spirit only, with a spiritual mindset.

These sinners you talk about, are living their lives, through their wants, needs, and desires. When this man lives in his mansion, does he feel the pleasure, can he enjoy his money? He may well create his desire to have such materialistic things around him, however, he will not be able to feel the rewards. Bricks and mortar cannot nourish one's soul.

One can only truly understand their worth by digging deep and living via soul needs. It is here that we value your true soul's worth; this is the currency you need to pay for things above and beyond your wildest dreams.

Now, should he tender a plant or give away a coin, then his soul will experience the joy. Therefore, he must learn to connect with that and continue to understand the life he has created is nothing more than an illusion.

Some will never stop trying to feed their needs, wants or desires and never do anything charitable, to experience their souls rejoice. Others that have lived a good life on earth, will instantly enjoy the pleasures of this world, like walking in the forest, breathing in the air. However, they must learn these again are needs: the need to stay close to their loved ones, the need to breathe, these are not necessary; they cannot serve your soul.

I hear your thoughts: is there a hell? This is a complex question, as those that reach this state of dimension have opened consciously or unconsciously to the possibilities of God. Those that cannot remain in the parallel dimension to you, until they are ready, or you and others alike, able them to see the light.

For some, their needs for either fear or punishment for their sins on earth will fall under their own wants, therefore they will create their own heaven, as they feel fit to suit. Hell may also be created by a good soul; however, their wants may expand to fear, self-judgment, self-punishment.

They may create a purposeful heaven fitting to their needs of negativity. This person is no unhappier than the man above, for your soul cannot feed off negativity, nor the joy of such mindful needs in this state of dimension.

This is a rebirth, another life that you must seek to understand, not all your rebirths are earthbound like you think. They must learn to overcome all desires, seeing that they carry no purpose to the soul. Not only are life lessons successfully passed on earth, referred to as rebirths, accepting love and light, by not surrendering to your weaknesses, allows that energy to give birth to your soul. You may have many rebirths in one's life.

—Guyirl

Until last night, I thought I had seen Heaven, like my 'street' which we each create, but all that has changed. My vision took me inside the church at the end of the street. On the podium stood the past minister of the church that I had attended. She was taking the service.

There were only a handful of people in the church ,and I was aware that her words were falling on deaf ears.

It saddened me that these people could not connect with such beauty. Pushing that aside, I sat listening to her beautiful service, when suddenly, I felt overpowered from within.

My soul ignited, and I literally burst open from within, flooding the church with light. The power of this force caused the walls of the church to collapse, leaving two huge twenty-foot wooden doors left standing unsupported. I can't remember walking through these doors, but do recall standing on the other side.

The beauty that stood before me was a little too much to take in. This new world opened up to me. No longer was my sight only capable of seeing the length of a street. My peripheral vision had disappeared, allowing me to see much further than any eyesight spectrum, I could have on this earth.

I witnessed mountains covered in snow; beaches, forests, lakes and temples, all within one glance, everything somehow united and celebrating the beauty with each other.

I watched as a coal miner walked by, with his tin lunch box in his hand, followed by a businessman, carrying his briefcase.

"Oh no, we don't still have to go to work up here, do we?" I asked myself. Such a random thought, but it happened.

On the same ground where the coal mine stood, an office block suddenly appeared instead. I realised that they were manifestations of their needs or wishes, to continue to work.

I don't normally believe in unicorns, but they were what came to my mind, as I stood there. This place was magical, perfect in every way. We could actually dream of the way we would like this world to be. Buildings that could disappear, mountains that could enjoy the beaches. Nothing makes sense here and yet, it was the most natural thing that I have witnessed.

I felt needed, loved, but most of all I felt at home.

Groups of children of all ages were marching, their energies full of fun, feeding a whole community. The elderly admired and respected by all, were worshipped for their knowledge.

Then, there were others, not in full colour, but deserving the right to be there, yet not quite ready to embrace such ideas. I couldn't judge them for this, I was over excited to want to watch them grow and change. The need to witness this development was like the pride felt when your child takes their first steps.

People started to flock towards me; it was quite overwhelming, to be honest. I felt like a timid puppy about to be showered with love and kisses from animal lovers. Sadly, my vision ended.

I have thought long and hard about my street, I now see that the man sitting waiting for his wife was not willing to move forward until she came home. The man in the bank vault held onto his materialistic desires and the man in his fishing boat was content with his own peace.

None of these people had found the compassion or love in their hearts to connect with the bigger picture of wanting to grow, learn and connect with their spirit or soul. It was hopefully, only a matter of time before they too would learn from the minister in the church and move on.

CHAPTER 14: MR BLACK

Three years ago, two girlfriends and I had gone along to a paranormal night, more for the entertainment aspect, than anything else. I apologize for that attitude, now having a better understanding of it all.

I was aware I had an ability to sense spirit, but was always too frightened to try. At the start of the evening, we were invited to join the other people, to open up and tune into our senses. It was the first time for me, but I could follow it, as I had heard a little about chakras, the light and visualization.

The evening was fun until we walked into the west wing of this listed building. The atmosphere became icy cold and more demanding of my attention than any of the other rooms. My sixth sense kicked in, consuming me with a chilling intensity. White noise filled my ears, together with the thunderous sound of my own heartbeat, jackhammering away.

It was there that I saw the shadow of a man, walking around the edge of the room. I was quite struck by his aura. I had never seen someone's aura before and it wasn't as I had expected. Apart from the fact that it was black, it was pixelated into blocks of tiny black squares arranged into different patterns, all surrounding him and giving off a dense vapor. I felt I could have written my name on it. This was where the name 'Mr Black' came from.

He looked over at us for a brief moment, totally disinterested in what we were doing and continued to walk, whilst muttering some nasty comments which were directed at us. I can't remember his words now, but I did repeat them to the other girls, at the time.

Mr Black seemed to be caught off guard by the fact that I could hear him. He turned and walked closer to me, his energy becoming stronger and more menacing. Suddenly, a wave of panic hit me hard, as his eyes became riveted onto mine. Goosebumps crawled across my flesh.

I inwardly cursed, to which he smiled a sardonic smile, an acknowledgment that he could hear me. Laughing, he repeated my curse. His laughter vanished, just as rapidly as it had erupted.

He waited for me to make my next move, commanding me with his presence to talk to him, but despite the invitation, my instincts knew better and we hastily left the wing.

I had to fight hard not to fall apart completely, for the sake of my friends and because I didn't want to sound like a raving lunatic, I continued the rest of the session, acting as nonchalantly as I could. The evening had started so innocently. I really should have known better, this was the very reason why I never allowed myself to open up to the supernatural.

During the three days following the Mr. Black incident, I wasn't myself. It may well have been only a fleeting contact with him, but he had left quite an impression on me.

A couple of years later, I was at the church, when I noted the following in my diary.

Diary Entry 17th May 2016
Last week, I learned something new, something I had never given a thought to and was shocked that it was accepted in the Spiritualist Church. Peter, our tutor, said that he would like to touch on a subject, that one of the group was very interested in. That was, "rescue work". I wondered what kind of rescue work it was: for animals, people or something else? He explained that it was for trapped souls, souls that had not moved on after passing. I must have turned white, as my biggest fear, which held my development back, was the thought of ghosts.

Peter told us he did a little bit of work in this area and explained that once he goes to meet a trapped soul, the first step is to communicate. For most souls, this is a wonderful thing as no one can normally hear them or talk to them. He briefly said how he sends them onto the Spirit World, with the power of love.

Over the next few days, I thought a lot about this, and it reminded me of Mr. Black's situation. Something I didn't ever want to talk about in the church, as I felt like I had done something really childish, but it has made me feel more compassion and love for this trapped man, even though he was no gentleman, nevertheless, I spent the last few nights sending him love and will continue to do so in my prayers.

End of post

For the next week, I sent out nothing but love and light, hoping it was full of potential and possibilities in helping Mr. Black pass to the Spirit World.

Diary Entry 25th May 2016

Last night, I went to the Spiritualist Church development and awareness group. It was very interesting and the topic was on love. We had to talk about our experiences of love and what unconditional love meant to us. I was the last to speak and having listened to everyone's opinions about their love for animals, partners, and the universe, my thoughts took me to the actual feelings of love.

I was aware of three feelings of love; firstly, my paid job as a wedding chauffeur. Most of the time, I feel the tremendous energy of love between the bride and groom. I have also been touched by a lady, who came to view and book one of my cars this week, this lady was covered in tattoos and piercings. At first sight, I wouldn't have thought that I could be so comfortable around her. I was wrong, the energy from her was so loving and kind, I had a lovely connection with her and I can't wait for her wedding, which takes place in a few weeks. So, my first feeling of love, is the special energy that I get from others.

The second feeling was that of unconditional love; the love I have for my boys, my dog and my husband (in that order, I write this, with my tongue in cheek). I, like most of you, would feel there is no stronger love than a Mother's love. I love my boys more than anything else and would die for them, if I had to. This to me is the second feeling of unconditional love.

Thirdly, this type of love, I have only been blessed to feel twice in my life. The power of God's love is like nothing I have ever experienced before. The second time I felt this was regarding the message that I received from Robert. Once I walked over the bridge, I felt God's love once again. I find it hard to say, but the highest of love on this earth, unconditional love or a mother's love is nothing, compared to God's love.

Having just read my last post, I can see I have been sending Mr. Black love, however, writing the comment about him not being gentle, shows that I have judged him, and my love had conditions. I must learn from this.

End of post

Before I had grasped the understanding of unconditional love, I suppose my intentions of sending Mr. Black love didn't carry much clout. Once my intentions were more sincere, and I removed the conditions, they carried more weight.

I had fallen asleep one night, my husband next to me in the bed, when a presence engulfed me. Fear gripped my whole body. Every part of my brain was screaming for me to reach out or scream to my husband.

Something invisible was on top of me, pinning me down. I was completely frozen in fear. I wanted to lash out, to fight for my life, but I was nothing more than a helpless rag doll. I laid there and suddenly a dark shadow, no longer shapeless, morphed into a face, just inches from mine. Fierce, feral-like eyes, surrounded by a network of angry red veins, pulsated on his face, threatening to burst at any minute.

His nostrils flared, mirroring his anger, his mouth opened wide and I felt his powerful breath wash over my skin, his rotten breath turned my stomach. An ear-shattering deep voice, screamed a long drawn out "FUCKKKK OFFFFF," cutting me to the bone with horror. Then he was gone.

Never in my life have I been so petrified or fearful of something out of my control. Those words will live in my veins forever.

For months, I put every ounce of my strength into resisting my thoughts from drifting, even resisting to connecting with my guides. I worried that allowing myself to open up, or tune in, would be taken by him, as permission to enter my thoughts or personal space.

Mr. Black never left my conscience; he hovered like a bad smell. I couldn't shake off the feeling that someone was watching me, simmering beneath the surface, ready to boil over at a moment's notice. Always ready, daring me to bring him closer. I was unable to cut the connection.

As time passed, the image of Mr. Black would uninvited, slip into my mind, instantly dropping the room temperature by ten degrees. However, his pixelated black boxes that surrounded him would change. Some disappeared altogether and some would become translucent. Slowly, I got used to him there, in the background, just observing me. Camaraderie was slowly beginning to develop. Those moments of vulnerability from him, started to dilute his hate, as my own fear diminished a little every day. There was an unspoken understanding, developing between us, one of curiosity.

I have no ending for Mr. Black. I feel he has chosen to prolong his punishment himself, maybe because he fears judgment on the other side. I do know he carries his earthly personality with him, including negative emotions, drama and probably fear. It leaves him earthbound in the fourth dimension.

He has left me on the one hand, very afraid of the future, feeling very alone and not knowing what I have to do. Information on the internet is quite conflicting and too little of it fits with my experiences. I will try to keep a brave face on things, but the gravity of what has happened this year has at times brought me to tears. There are many dangers attached to this job that I feel I must warn you about. Mr. Black's story is important and cannot, despite all my good intentions, be turned into a fairy-tale ending.

On the other hand, I am euphoric, having witnessed the beauty in successfully passing someone over. In a nutshell, the latter does outweigh the first, and that is what gives me the strength to carry on. Mr. Black has taught me the power of unconditional love.

It's been over a year since I wrote the heading 'Mr. Black.' I have never felt brave enough to sit and work on it until this weekend. Within a paragraph or two, I have scared myself half to death reliving my fears. I am currently sitting close to the door, one eye on my notepad and one eye on my dog. If he runs, I'm off, as well! That being said, I am not sure if outside is more frightening than being in here with Mr. Black.

I have waited a long time to understand the purpose of this book and to be shown a sign that everything in my head is real. It really can't be any clearer than the miracles or phenomena that are right in front of me outside, today.

It cannot be a coincidence that Mr. Black plays his part in this book. Today of all days, right before, not just my eyes, but most of the UK, we are witnessing the effects that the shadows or grounded spirits can and will have on our world, if we don't heed to the warnings.

Most of you reading this book will remember the sixteenth of October 2017; the day that the sun and sky shone blood red, from the Sahara desert sand blowing over the UK.

I have spent thirty years trusting and never doubting my signs. Yes, there is a scientific reason for today. Thirty years ago, to this day, there was the worst storm ever recorded in the UK. Am I overthinking this? Maybe to some, but never have I had such a powerful sign. What if I have just exposed the biggest threat to darkness, the solution on how we can remove grounded spirits? Would that not be powerful enough to send the darkness blood red? Over a year ago I wrote in my diary, dictated by my Spirit Guide:

I have felt strongly about a change coming. We can either wait and see if the change is for the worst, at our own peril or we unite to create the change. One day on the news they will announce a new light or a new atmosphere, this will be our evidence that we are working in the right direction. This is the proof we need that a new light will show us that we are working to make this world a better place.

—*Unknown*

I haven't been able to understand it until now. If you don't remember this day, then search on the internet: 16th October 2017.

Handbook Notes

You may not agree with me on this, but I have questioned my Guides, why would they allow Mr. Black to attack me? I have not been given an answer, however, I have always felt Mr. Black was an important part of this book and my learning.

The lesson I can give you is very important; protection, protection, protection. This work is not for the faint-hearted, (that being said, if I were to compare myself to anyone it would have to be Shaggy and Scooby-Doo.) This field of work must be done using all your training in grounding, protection and most of all, you must connect and work with your own guides. This connection must be strong and may require you to wait for a new guide or guides, who help in this field.

I could not do this without Doc's or Monk's help. I will remind you of a quote given to me.

Powerful energies are destined in bringing about this new dawn. Skilled workers unaware of their abilities are awakening to their destiny. Lightworkers far and wide must join in a united form to prevent this eclipse, your light must be so magnificent that the blind cannot ignore.

New spiritualism is old and advanced heightened awakening will lead the way forward.

A new era is possible via the ripples you and others create, tsunamis will destroy the darkness.

Do not underestimate the pinprick you leave. That one little ray of light that shines through is enough to free one person's soul that in return will remove the shadow that clouds other ones seeing. This must not be overlooked; you must go back to this in your script. You have been given groundbreaking sight, into a plight that will have a tremendous effect. You are now more than just the pen.

—Guyirl

CHAPTER 15: CLASSROOMS

There have been a few moments in my life when I find spiritual clarity. Seconds when I can recall the whole purpose and reasons for not only this world, but for a parallel world. I can awaken as my true spiritual soul. It's either a recall, waking up to things beyond my knowledge, or I have stepped into their world for a brief moment. Am I able to tell you any of it? No. The problem is like I am living in a world of non-reality, controlled by a higher force that wipes clean my memory as quickly as I register the truth; it's like someone is hitting the memory delete button, over and over again.

I try to grab the thoughts, feelings and knowledge that I briefly experience as they fade away, leaving me knowing something, yet nothing. It is this nothingness of something that I am trying to pull for information, regarding dimension.

It is happening more frequently, since I have asked for understanding of the dimensions. Quite often, they come with awful physical efforts, I call them 'mind shifts'. It is like being on a roller coaster and feeling dizzy and travel sick. It is not a pleasant experience and it will wake me up leaving me feeling ill, for a few moments. The scariest thing of all happens when something in my head makes a very loud snapping noise. I really feared that perhaps I had a brain tumour and everything that I have experienced, spiritually, was the tumour causing hallucinations. That was before I got this following message:

Your mind is expanding with everything we do, I see the physical effects it has on you and we monitor you closely. Wisdom will come at a price and you must choose to allow this in your waking state. No danger can be placed on you. However, in joining us, you will experience vibrations that will be uncomfortable for a while.

Monks spend a lifetime training; this is not an easy task.

We are embracing you with this, we hope that you share this knowledge. This is a blessing higher than most will seek. We see your potential, hence the work we are putting in while you sleep. You may stop this at any time, but we have sought to unite our two planes for some time and your willingness will bring us closer.

—Eve

So what can I pull from my knowing of nothing? If I had Penny to help I could fly through this chapter, but Penny left me these parting words some time ago:

It is with a heavy heart that I step back today, but on a plus, I get to stand back and admire your work. I know you now understand my need for silence. You are strong enough to carry your concerns on your own, to use all the knowledge we have given you to complete this book.

Follow your own truth and convictions within your soul. Your voice is now stronger than mine and carries life experience.

Do not worry about those blinded by fear, unable to understand the true meaning of this book. For every three that cannot open their hearts, you will have one that does. That is such a breakthrough in our quest.

Never in such an unhealthy state, as your world needed or requested such a radical change. Own your quest and stand proud, for if you shy away from the truth, how can you expect others to stand tall?

Write from your heart, I am so proud, and will continue to look over your shoulder."

Penny

The title of this chapter was, originally, 'Dimensions.' However, I am no scholar nor scientist; I am simply a loving mother and a good wife, and a useless housewife, of course, but I would never claim to be perfect!

I really don't want to talk about something that many others already have. I don't have the clarity, especially now that Penny has stepped back. So, I am going to strike out the word, 'dimensions' and refer to them as 'The University.' The classrooms are as follows:-

- **1st** - The 1st is the earth, the minerals, plants and so on.
- **2nd** - The 2nd connects with animals, the basic needs for survival.
- **3rd** - The 3rd is us, our ability to create, to think, using a superior mind to that of the second.
- **4th** - The 4th, this is where I feel extremely confident that I do understand and that I have visited this dimension. That said, I didn't actually have to go anywhere. In the fourth dimension our world is shared with grounded spirits; they are earthbound. This dimension is responsible for the darkness, as a result of their evil intentions, tormented state of being, fear of faith or worst of all being held prisoner. Not all of them are negative, for instance, remember Betty in a previous chapter; she was earthbound through her love for Edward, but sadly she also contributes to the darkness.
- **5th** - The 5th is the street I see in heaven, however, if you remember that had two sides. Those to the left of the church, where the man sat indoors and the man in the bank vault, etc. All these people hadn't realised that they had died, nor had

they found the faith to connect with their own spirits. I am so pleased that I saw these people on the same level as the ones past the church doors. None of these people were less desiring to be in heaven than those that did have faith.

- **6th** - This was the street behind the church doors. This one was beautiful, a perfect world that we could only dream of. Yet, still there was a lot of spiritual growth to be done here. In order to graduate from this room, we need to do one of two things, or more than likely both, and that is to release all our ties with our loved ones, here on earth and in the 5th or 6th classrooms, or having been given permission to be released from our loved ones, whom have kept us close. We can't do any of this without accepting that we are ready to truly die, to give up life as we know it and realise that we are just spirit, willing to then let go of all our own wants, needs and desires for our own benefit and dedicate our existence purely to others.

- **7th** - So what have I seen of the 7th classroom? It is here that we no longer have human form, we have surrendered to everything we know; the need to eat, breathe, walk and talk, verbally of course. We accept that we are just energy made up of love and light. This is pulled from my experience from my beautiful red foxes (the Shamans).

Now that we are pure and free from our human brains, and incapable of ever needing anything for ourselves, except the desire to serve. We are put to work. Not educated enough to be a guide as yet, this is where our classrooms in the universe comes in. Our lessons learned are recalled and our next exams are planned.

I woke up the next morning after writing this chapter, not remembering a dream, but knowing that this is just one layer of the 7th classroom and it was important to go back and weigh up my evidence, with my experiences.

There have been many times when crossings have been straightforward, like the time I was busy folding clothes, when a man with his leg in plaster appeared and asked for help. I reassured him that he didn't need the plaster and I would be his crutch. This was all that was needed, as he ran for the light, leaving his plaster cast behind.

Another time, an elderly lady asked for help to find her cat. Out of the corner of my eye, I saw Monk standing in the light, cat in arms. I pointed in his direction, she thanked me and crossed over through the light.

I am not really sure regarding the reasons for one not entering the light at their moment of death, or indeed the part that I should play. My opinion is I am needed to bring forward the light, together with Doc and Monk's help, when the time is right and they are ready to cross over.

I mentioned earlier about the time I saw my soul standing in front of me. Apart from the lesson I needed to learn, it was the ending that now seems to have the greatest importance. My soul was in the outline of a human; I felt the strong urge to conform to a small orb. It is this orb that reminds me of the light that appears at each crossing. Witnessing this leads me to think that the light is made up of thousands, if not millions of tiny orbs, each orb being one divine spirit's soul. It would make sense to me that such a grand effort of so many would be needed to create a passage.

The reason why both divine spirit and I team up is to ensure the job is done in the moment the earthbound spirit gives over their free will. If this was not the case, would the light in which they cross over not be constantly available for them?

Referring back to the case of Betty to validate this theory, my experience was, there was no light, and for Samuel's crossing, (to come), I had to call for the light. More evidence for the light not being present with them, the whole time.

So what is the light? Surely if it was just that of a torch or beam, it would take no energy of love to be a constant thing. If like the orb, I witnessed being just one spiritual soul, it would take both teamwork and commitment to play a part. That in mind, I believe now, that this is what is referred to as the 'Channel of Love.' The more I write, the clearer it feels, as if I have the answer.

The visions I have been given, showing what heaven looks and feels like, are wonderful. In a nutshell, heaven is whatever you want it to be. However, I don't want to shatter this promise; this is your personal heaven and not the true heaven.

When we choose to move from this world to the next plane, there is a knowing and understanding that there is no pain, being apart from our loved ones.

We move from here to the spiritual university, to educate ourselves. The setup is very much like the classrooms we have here in the real world.

It has struck me that the word 'university' is connected with the word 'universe.' The universe is our higher plane, where once we set foot inside, all becomes clear, and we must let go of all our attachments to earthly things, including people.

Once we enter this classroom, it becomes clear that our many lives on this earth are just lessons. All our lessons, from all our previous lives, flood back to us. This, for some, is euphoric, although the memory is swiftly deleted.

Knowing and understanding that the part we have just played was just like a character in a film may be, for some, a realization which hurts: they are not willing or able to let go of love or other connections without retaining attachments.

When this is the case, we are reborn, not as children, but sent back as God's creatures, great or small. This allows all attachments to be removed, responding only to our instincts for survival. The length of time that the creature lives depends on the strength of our attachments.

Once this is complete, we return to the classroom, never forgetting our connections or memories, but healthy and free enough, to continue to move on to our next life, mapping out our own path, knowing the lesson/exam we must successfully master, in order to graduate, to become a Spirit Guide.

Don't forget, if this is upsetting for you and you don't want to detach yourself from the people that you love, you are free to stay in your own Heaven.

Soul mates

As my vision has validated, once in heaven, I cannot feel or show more love for my husband or child than a stranger, however, that said, we do meet souls on the same development level of understanding and purity with ourselves, as we do on the earth. We also hold on to our personalities, that attract like for like.

Our soul mates travel with us from the classroom to our earthly life, not always as our husband or wife, sometimes it can be a friend or stranger you meet that you just know and feel a connection or familiarity with, or best of all, the connection with a pet. Should one fail at a task, you may find that sadly, one person moves on until hopefully, they catch up or you are sent back to help.

Likewise, if you feel you don't want to be in your Heaven with your earthly husband and you feel you have no ties, then you go straight to the classroom, but remember, if your husband creates his heaven with you in it, this becomes another exam. You willingly, with love and clear understanding, play a role in educating him, so at his '5pm' or expected moment, you return to his heavenly setting. (Remember 5pm may not exist).

Now that I have told you my truth, you may need to ask yourself, what it is in this life you must learn or overcome. Are you a victim? Are you a bully? Has life been unkind? Are you insecure or selfish? Do you get stressed too easily? Have anxiety over the pressures to succeed? Whatever it is, it must be remembered that unless you resolve these problems and difficulties, during your lifetime on earth, you will relive this over and over again in subsequent lives, not necessarily with the same people, but the scenario will be the same.

What if life has been cruel on more than one occasion? Then, allow yourself to believe that you are strong; strong enough to have set yourself several goals in one lifetime.

Do you want to fail? Do you really want to relive this life? If the answer is no, then now is the time to detach yourself from feeling like a victim or a prisoner to your negativity. Whatever the problem is in your life, do whatever it takes to pass this exam. Support groups are out there for all situations, pick up that phone and tell yourself, *I'm not going through this again in my next life*. Set your goal high, don't just pass, earn a distinction. Conquer your troubles and learn your lesson, then help others conquer theirs.

Maybe you are rich and famous, and see this as happiness? But remember, it is only this world that recognizes richness as happiness. What if your life is normal, with no major events, are you just an extra? Prior to this year, I very much felt that this was the case for me, until I decided to go looking for my task.

I do believe we can get breaks from lessons, but maybe your lesson is to write that book, do voluntary work, find your faith, help me with my quest to rescue our loved ones. *So, what if you're not a medium or a healer?* I hear you say. All you need is faith and love. Join a spiritual circle; your energy is no less important than mine or anyone else's.

Now, ask your guide if there is truth in this. If you can't hear them, ask your soul, and search within. Does this ring true? Is there a stirring in your soul? Does it fit like a glove on your hand, or a second skin around you? Are the hairs on your arms sticking up, or shivers going down your back? If the answer is yes, then deep down, your soul is jumping for joy, as you are now starting to see life for what it is. Pass with distinction.

CHAPTER 16: SAMUEL

I lay in bed, recalling the lovely energy I had enjoyed at the church service the day before, when I felt myself drifting deeply. The room began to slip sideways. Soon, I was standing in a forest. Everything seemed so still and peaceful, as I watched the early evening draw in, the haze of the golden sun highlighting the lovely contour of the forest trees ahead of me.

I enjoy my visions, especially if there is no time significance attached to them, or I go to visit new places.

A rush of seriousness suddenly hit me, causing the elation of the cool warm evening to fade. A heavy, threatening atmosphere brought my attention to a frantic commotion behind me. Hurried footsteps, crunching through the forest floor, raced towards me as

I caught sight of a tall, heavily-built man, hurtling closer. Rugged and outdoorsy, he looked to be in his mid-thirties, with curly black hair plastered with sweat to his lovely chocolate-brown face. He slowed as he approached me.

"Please, let me help you. What's your name?" I asked.

"Samuel, Mam," his exhausted voice replied. It was the way he addressed me that instantly made me realise I had gone back in time.

His puffy, tearless eyes held mine, as I continued to stare back, hoping his face would provide me with the answers. I needed to understand what was happening here and to make sense of the situation. The fear spread all over his face, told me he didn't expect my sympathy or love, that was clear.

Now, lost in the wilderness, the gradual increase in the level of darkness behind him started to consume me. It felt as if a terrifying, destructive storm was approaching.

The once sweet sky was now overcast and grey, and I could see beams of torch lights flickering from afar. As they got closer, they started to reveal the source heading towards us.

I had stepped into a piece of living hell, evil history. It didn't take more than a second to identify their white full-length gowns, masks with eye slits and pointed hats. Liquid fear froze me to the spot, as I counted at least ten beams hitting me like the impact of a truck.

An ear-shattering scream brought my attention back to Samuel. Searching for the origin of that scream, I was shocked to find that the noise had come from me. I battled to find my focus, as a new terror took instant possession, and a sense of imminent doom consumed me.

A thousand things ran through my mind. Of course, I voiced none of them. I didn't have to try too hard to push these aside, or avoid contemplating the awful scenario. My body was no longer willing to wait for a command, it took on its own self-preservation instinct for survival as Samuel and I ran.

I was terrified by the speed at which we were running, disoriented, and trembling. I pressed a hand to my racing heart, suddenly my foot hit something hard, causing me to fall to my hands and knees. I let out a cry, I could go no further. Samuel stopped, I could see he was torn, did he come back to help me, knowing it could possibly be at the expense of his own life?

Samuel turned and slumped down beside me. My heart bled for him intensifying our bond. We were a tangled mess of arms and legs, as we held each other tight. I cursed myself for not being able to continue. Breathing deep into my lungs, I recognized the energy of Doc and Monk pouring through my veins.

I yelled aloud "Show me the light," upon which my guides answered my panicked plea.

To the right of me shone God's calling. Samuel jumped up in a panic. In my stupidity, I had forgotten the very thing that he was running away from, and now, it seemed to be right on top of us. He had mistaken the light for that of the torches close by.

"Monk, please," I screamed desperate for help, heartbroken to see the dejected Samuel wanting to run in the other direction.

Monk's response was immediate, clear and instructive. In the distance, a soft white glow highlighted a little white church. Samuel didn't need further instruction; he was off, heading towards the sound of the congregation singing in absolute harmony, in a perfect place, where he would find safety.

"God bless, God bless," I repeated over and over, as Samuel ran into the church.

Relieved that Samuel was now safe, palms held together in front of my chest, I lifted my head whilst still continuing to praise the Lord. My vision blurred for a few seconds, before the whole world went white.

Above me, hanging from the branches of the trees, hung dead, tortured bodies of all ages, for as far as my eyes could see. I threw my hands up to my mouth, and tears streamed down my face as panic and terror flooded through me.

The pure shock of this image thankfully brought me back to the safety of my own bed. I was shocked to feel that my face mirrored the horror in my vision. Curling into a fetal position, I hugged the pillow to muffle my cries.

Something tugged at the corner of my mind. Debbie, the tutor at the development group and the circle I attended. I snatched my attention back.

Suddenly, the enormity of the situation dawned on me.

Despite having no professional training regarding crossing overs, I also knew I was no beginner, and there was no one else I could call on. Everything was telling me, for the first time, that this was hazardous to my health and certainly my mental wellbeing, but still I chose to close my eyes and return.

"Doc, Monk, please, flood me with light and with every ounce of my soul, let me burst with love," I pleaded.

My guides and I gave everything we had to give. Slowly, we started to turn the dark forest floor into a pool of light. Raising this energy took all the strength we had. I fought hard to tap into the power deep within, unaware that my physical body could hold so much.

I knew this was to be the biggest challenge I would ever have to partake in, and to a level I had never experienced before. My head dangerously threatened to burst, as we continued to push even harder. Slowly we managed to raise the light, until we had reached the top of the tree line and our work was done.

God bless, Samuel and friends.

Handbook Notes

Would I do it again? In a heartbeat. Would I *want* to do it again? Never. Something inside me has died as a result of that experience. I can't tell you what it is, or whether it is physical or mental, but in my perfect, safe little life, here on Earth, having never experienced such evil, I find it too traumatic to continue on my own.

The image of the circle in my church that I saw played heavily on my mind, it was their help that I needed, in sharing the burden and also for creating the power of love that was needed. Fortunately, I managed the task with Doc's and Monk's help, but not without any after-effects, as I still get flashbacks.

My only wish is that we could do this within the safety of the church, sharing the burden with like-minded people. I did get a lovely message from Guyirl as follows (From the sounds of it, I must have been moaning about the lack of contact, at the time).

"Greetings O deaf one. You have come such a long way to question our voices. There is always a reason for absence, but you must feel content that we are always with you.

The teachings we convey upon you carry responsibilities, hence why we must be sure that you are ready to listen.

Blessed are you that we share the knowledge you seek, but this must be written correctly. You are doing well and you must praise yourself for your commitment.

Trust in us as you have, and together we will fill others with love and light. I am proud of you, my love, for the rescue of Samuel and others. I can assure you that they are all safe and well, surrounded by the kindness one deserves. Keep up the good work.

—Guyirl

CHAPTER 17: CONTRACT

IN 2017, I witnessed something so remarkable that I thought not only had I been given the ending of this book, but also been shown my new purpose, a new way to look at my work. I need to go back and tell you briefly about Jenny, a lady that I met over ten years ago.

Sometimes we meet people in our lives that we just feel a connection with. I first met Jenny at a conference. We talked briefly and felt a connection. Over the next ten years, thanks to Facebook, I would see her pop up and from afar get to know bits of her life or new business adventure. I would always comment and wish her well.

I bumped into her again a couple of years ago, and she informed me of her latest project: she was setting up as a funeral director. Absolutely stunned, I wished her well yet again.

In January of 2017, a good six months after our last meeting, I received a message from her saying she might have a business proposition for me. We arranged to meet the following day. The local Spiritualist Church had an open afternoon and I had decided to go along there after my meeting with Jenny.

As we talked, it became clear to me that this wasn't about business, and when she started talking about fate, we moved on to spiritualism. No business deal was offered, but I invited her to join me at the church. Needless to say, she was given a message from her mother, who had passed over, that was very much needed at that time. Well done, guides.

In April 2017, three months after this, I received a text message from Jenny: *Are you free for a coffee?* We had not seen each other since that one meeting in January.

Sure, is everything alright? I responded.

Yes, I have a business offer for you, I will explain it tomorrow. Jenny went on to say that a tender for the council had come and gone. Later, she had received an email from them, asking why she hadn't put in for the tender, adding that they were reopening applications.

This was where I was needed. The contract was to supply two private ambulances, and she didn't have the funds. She also explained that the moment she had received the email, I had come straight into her mind and stayed there.

I agreed to subcontract to her and find the money to purchase two more cars. I have to be honest, the request took a while to sink in, but when the penny dropped it hit me like an iron bar hitting a glass floor, I was speechless. There I was working at the hospital spiritually crossing people over, and here she was knocking on my door, asking me to physically transport hundreds of dead people to the mortuaries.

My mind was blown away. I hadn't told Jenny anything about my work of crossing people over, I had only told her that I did volunteer work. I have always worried that I can't reach as many people as I would like, to help to cross over. Being just a volunteer at this time, I was only in contact with very few dying people. If we received the contract, according to council figures, over three hundred souls a year would be forwarded my way. Now, tell me that our paths are not laid out? Tell me that it's just a coincidence that an acquaintance knocks on my door and asks this of me?

On 10th May, we would find out if we had been blessed with the contract. In the meantime, I had been reading a book on how to set our intentions and how, by asking the universe for help, one can change one's life. *Silly me,* I thought. At midnight on Saturday night, I finished the book, and I put this to the test.

"I would like to ask the universe to help Jenny to get the contract, in order for me to supply vehicles to pick up one's loved ones."

At 12.10pm, my mobile phone rang.

"Hello, is this Jack's mum? He has passed out on the high street and we can't move him, can you come and get him? (He was drunk, of course).

At 12.15am, I was driving, going to pick up my comatose son's body. Now that's a lesson to be careful in what you wish for.

For the next few weeks, I couldn't stop thinking about the magnitude of this contract. Apart from supplying the vehicles, what role could I play? *Please, please, please, don't ask me to be a bearer,* I thought. Although I sit and watch people take their last breath, being called to traffic accidents, suicides, and the like were way out of my comfort zone. If those scenarios are out of the question, it is possible the vehicles themselves were to be involved. Maybe I am going to be shown how to bless the departed, or perhaps I can send my Guides, Doc and Monk, on every call out. Perhaps I could find bearers, from the church, who secretly pray and help. Maybe just by being given their names and addresses, I might be able to call on them and carry out a passing. Whatever happened, I knew it would become clear, but I knew in my heart and soul, this would be a way of passing over hundreds more souls every year.

Finally, it was May 9th, 2017. The next day, I would find out if we had the contract. *Tomorrow*, I thought, *I will find out whether God is entrusting me with possibly hundreds of beautiful souls, to guide them on their journey.* As I have already mentioned, I had no idea how this would play out and what role, if any, I would need to play.

CHAPTER 18: SISTER MARIA

Sister Maria, a ward sister, had served most of her working life in the same hospital, in which she now lay, waiting to pass.

It wasn't my first time sitting with Sister Maria. Over the course of a few weeks, I had got to know quite a lot about her, from the steady stream of co-workers whose lives she had not only touched, but had made a lasting effect. They all spoke about how she was a proud, independent woman who would want neither pity nor charity from anyone and most of all, how I was not to be fooled by her size. What she lacked in height, she made up in her presence, and boy, did she like to make her presence known.

Sister Maria was known for being sterner than most, and was referred to as the backbone of the hospital, a figure of authority. Respected and admired, yet also feared by most. Above and beyond her duties, her patience and unconditional love were limitless. She had dedicated her life to her job and sadly never found her life partner.

She wasn't going to have to wait much longer for her cruel illness to end. Medication had relieved her painful breathing, but now it was a waiting game. She needed to give herself permission to leave this world.

Spiritually, I felt completely disconnected. I was completely unable to intrude on anyone's privacy unless invited. All I needed was the offer of her hand. Yet, when we did touch, it felt like a bolt of electricity passing between us. She recoiled, making it known that I wasn't needed. It was the first time I'd felt useless, with nothing to offer.

I sat reading her one of her favourite books, a Mills and Boon love story. Outside the side room, there was quite a bustle of activity going on: Saturday evenings have always been a busy time. A cold draft of air swept in from the hallway, as two nurses walked by. I overheard the tail-end of a conversation, regarding an attempted suicide, and sent a silent prayer.

All of a sudden, the room changed. An energy, radiating love and purity, seemed to envelop me. Sparks of light twinkled like diamond facets in the sun, filling every nook and cranny in the four walls. The sparks united and formed one incredibly powerful sphere, brighter than anything I had ever seen before, almost blinding, yet pleasing to look at. The sphere then split into three parts. All the joys of the universe filled me, as I sat looking at three winged angels, I was captivated by their beauty.

They were not luminescent, but gleaming; the closest I can get to describing the colour was a bright mother-of-pearl. Their wings looked and sounded like cloth, but feathery, above perfection. They all wore the outline of past nursing uniforms, all different, in keeping with their own historical time periods. Vibrating with their own signature energy, each of them unique, ageless and beautiful.

Studying them, I tried to engrave everything I was seeing and feeling onto my brain. I was being blessed, witnessing such a powerful thing. It was as though I had found the Holy Grail and was drinking from it: a flavour so rich, I wanted to savour it forever. I could have lingered there for quite some time, but I had to come back to reality.

Unaware I had closed my eyes, I opened them just in time to see Sister Maria's spirit leave her body and unite with her angels. Except unite she did not. I was totally caught off guard, as Sister Maria walked right past the angels and left the room. Caught in the surreal moment, I gathered my wits. I had to get the situation under control as quickly as possible. I had a feeling the angels wouldn't be able to stay for long.

I just caught the back of Sister Maria, as she walked behind a closed cubicle in the main ward.

Diane, one of the nurses I had spoken to earlier, walked past,

"Diane, I'm sorry to say Sister Maria has just passed." I gave her a moment to reflect.

"Is everything alright? I overheard a comment earlier about a lady." I asked.

Diane pointed to the closed cubicle. "Yes, we have a young girl. The police are trying to locate the family," she scrunched up her nose, it was a tell-tale sign that it didn't look very promising.

"Would you mind if I sat a while with her, until the family gets here?" I hoped my face hid my real reason for why I needed to speak to Sister Maria.

"Ros, that will be lovely if you can spare us the time. We have her monitored. I will see to Sister Maria."

As I entered the cubicle, Sister Maria was in front of me. She was leaning over the young girl. For your benefit and maybe mine too, I will spare you the truly gory details about the young woman. Looking beyond her injuries, was a strikingly beautiful young woman, I would guess no older than thirty years of age. Tears stung the corner of my eyes, but I refused to let them fall. What this poor girl must have gone through, to try to end such a precious life, was beyond me.

Sister Maria turned her attention to the monitor. I'm not a nurse, but I saw that her vital signs were not good. Her heart rate was falling dramatically. I ran to call a nurse, just as Diana and the team re-entered. Slowly, they seemed to fade into the background, their voices muted by the deafness of the silence, as the three angels returned.

I watched as Sister Maria swept her arms under the girl's lifeless body and lifted her soul upwards. Seconds later, all three angels gathered around. Each of them linking hands and spreading their wings, creating a light that shone high above them. A strange power came coursing through the ward, more powerful and pure than anything I'd ever experienced before.

Sister Maria, with the girl still in her arms, rose up and left the room.

God bless, Sister Maria and the young woman.

Handbook Notes

I feel extremely privileged to have been able to witness the beauty of the passing of Sister Maria. Not only was I blessed with both seeing and feeling the pure beauty of the presence of not one, but three angels; I also witnessed the most unselfish thing I have experienced and now strive to do this myself, to rescue another.

Despite the fact that this was Sister Maria's moment of crossing over, being the person she was in life, she continued to carry that with her into her passing, putting another person's needs before her own.

I know we have seven principles within the SNU Church. However, if ever an eighth was needed, it would be in honour of Sister Maria: this need to rescue another. It could be taken as an example of either rescue work within the living or the deceased. I will hold my eighth principle now for the rest of my life; it lives in her honour.

CHAPTER 19: CIRCLE

As you can imagine, the final week was filled with what if's, leading up to that closing date regarding the council contract. Sadly, it turned out that we didn't get the contract, and although that wasn't a problem, I struggled to figure out why I had felt such a powerful spiritual connection with this. I was upset that I was only helping one person at a time, and that would never be enough, in my mind.

If Mohammed won't go to the mountain, we will send the mountain to Mohammed. Although my experiences had started to show that more than one soul could be rescued at a time, it upset me a great deal that there could have been extra help with the contract.

When the news came through, I was in the North of England, visiting my family. A few days later, I had been invited to attend a closed circle at the Spiritualist Church, run by my sister. Lately, they had found as a group that they were assisting in helping to pass over grounded souls. This had not been the intention of the circle, but it was becoming more frequent.

Ten of us sat in the circle and linked into spirit. Together, as a group, they started to build a picture. One person visualised the word, Mauritania, on a ship's life-belt. Another followed, describing a chef, but this man was connected to the Lusitania, its sister ship. The scene built up to be a bit like the tragedy of the Titanic. Another person picked up pains in the leg from the cook, who was trapped in a ship's galley. Images continued, and together they built up the message. When I say they worked together, I watched, as one word confirmed or finished off another person's sentence. I can only explain it this way, if I were to see a red door for instance within the image, it would be someone else who would speak of the red door, before I did. This was proof that we were all linked in.

As the evening progressed, it became apparent that we were doing a rescue for a ship's cook, trapped in the kitchen. Once that was completed, a woman appeared trapped on another ship, followed by a man who worked on the docks. There was a strong link, which had all started with just one word, "Mauritania."

I was there to witness their work, freeing this man, asking spirit to move the object that had pinned him, I listened as they spoke to the lady, who had died and guided her to the vortex of light, that they had worked hard to create between them.

However, just as this was happening, I saw a sky full of what looked like raining white petals, I instantly dismissed them, anxious to get back to witnessing the lady crossover to the Spirit World, which I did, but, again the raining petals returned. I was slightly annoyed, thinking for a moment that perhaps I was getting a crossed message to pass on, until one of the girls said that she could see many more jumping into the vortex. My image came back stronger and clearer, as I witnessed again, the sky full of not white petals, but lost souls: hundreds, if not thousands of them.

I had mistaken them for petals, but this time, looking closer, they were in fact souls going up to the sky, thousands of trapped souls, all jumping into the energy that the members of the circle had provided. I was on cloud nine to have witnessed this. I had been saddened that we failed to get the contract. If Jenny had got it, possibly hundreds of souls could have been rescued, yet, here I was witnessing what one loving circle had the potential to do.

At the closing of the circle, they searched on the internet. The Lusitania was torpedoed by a German U-boat, in May 1915, during the First World War. We carried out this rescue in May 2017.

Mauretania was not only the sister ship to the Lusitania. Mauritania is also the name of a ship's graveyard in the sea, off the west coast of Africa. It is the largest ship graveyard in the world; over three hundred rotting ships have come to rest there. From 2013, shipping companies from around the world are still sending old ships on their final voyage, to the Mauritania site.

All in all, that lovely circle called for anyone trapped within any ship to pass, and I was blessed to see it. It made it less painful to lose the council contract and the possibility of recovering three hundred lost souls.

The previous chapter was meant to be the end of this book. My plan was to leave you in suspense as to whether I got the contract or not. I felt happy writing it up this way, until we received the disappointing news that we hadn't been successful. I didn't want to mislead you at all. That being said, I feel it's relevant to leave it in, as I still feel a nagging suspicion that it is not over, that something would come of either the contract, or Jenny's funeral business. Time will tell.

Regarding the contract, both my mother and sister believed that certain things in life cannot be altered by spirit, and it was a case of not what you know, but, who you know in this circumstance. I have decided that although I am convinced this is not the end of the matter, I will put it aside and carry on with my book.

Update 2020: I was offered this business for sale. Sadly, we didn't have the funds available.

CHAPTER 20: NURSE CINDY

I had never known traffic like it for a Wednesday, making what should have been a twenty-minute journey to work become an hour's drive. When I managed to find the only space left in the car park, I headed up to B3 ward, to sit vigil with Miss Doris Millen.

Pushing through the doors, I walked over to the empty desk and waited for a nurse. I looked around to see Cindy, a young nurse I had met a few times before and was very fond of. She was walking out from behind a closed curtain. I smiled at her and the elderly lady that stood behind her. Cindy only returned the gesture.

"Hi Ros, are you here for Doris?" she asked.

"Yes, I'm sorry, the traffic was awful," I replied.

I gestured over to the closed curtains, assuming that's where I would be heading

"Come into the office for a minute," her tone giving away what was to follow.

"I'm sorry Ros, Doris has just passed ten minutes ago, but don't worry, she was not alone, I was able to sit with her," she shone with pride.

I sat and listened, trying so hard to keep eye contact with Cindy and not look at the lady standing by her side. My mind was racing, what should I do? I couldn't tell her that Doris was standing behind her, I couldn't ask to go and sit with Doris's body, to see if I could try to connect.

"I'm sorry, Ros, are you okay?"

"Yes, I'm just annoyed at the traffic, but, I'm glad you were with her. Do you think I could stay for coffee? It is best that I let the rush hour pass." A perfect response to stall for time, whilst I tried to conjure a plan.

"Sure. I will join you, I am overdue a break," she sighed.

I watched as the two of them left the office and re-entered with Cindy carrying the hot drinks.

We sat a while chatting casually.

"Do you remember the first time I met you in the ICU and you said you were a soul midwife. I thought you had come to the wrong ward, I was about to direct you to the maternity ward," she laughed.

"Sorry, Cindy, I'm miles away. Yes, I remember the look of confusion on your face. I bet I didn't look too good either. That was my first vigil; truth be known, I was petrified. Was it a gentle passing with Doris?" I hoped that last comment would get Doris's attention.

"It was peaceful as can be expected. She wasn't, shall we say, one of the easiest patients to work with, but she took a shine to me: called me Suzy, thinking I was her granddaughter. Sweet really, I had a soft spot for her. I better get back to work."

I left the ward, confused. Whilst standing in the corridor, I mentally called out Doris's name, to see if I could get her to come to me, sadly I couldn't and left.

For weeks after the incident, I would call into the B3 ward to say hello, but Cindy was never there. One of her fellow nurses had said she was off sick.

Six weeks passed, and then one day, whilst I was grocery shopping, I heard a voice from behind me.

"Hi, Ros." I turned and didn't recognize the young woman for a second, but I sure recognized Doris, standing beside her.

"Hi, Cindy, how are you? They said you had been off work." Poor Cindy, she was half the size I remembered, not that she could afford to lose any weight. Despite her makeup, she looked dreadful. "You still don't look well; no offense."

"None taken, I haven't been good, having the tests done as we speak, but I just have no energy. They put me on antidepressants because I keep crying. Are you still going up to the hospital?"

"Yes. Listen, why don't you pop round to mine for coffee?" I asked.

"Thanks Ros, but I am not good company at the minute. Sorry, I must go," and off she went, Doris following suit.

For weeks after this, I sent out love and light to Doris and asked my guides to help in any way they could. I had no idea what else I could do, without jeopardizing my job at the hospital. I had to weigh up if being honest with Cindy was worth the risk of not being able to help the many call outs, at the hospital.

I have never before read a book on spiritualism, purely because I have to be a hundred percent sure that what comes in my untrusting mind, is given by my Guides and not a thought recalled from someone else's experiences. That being said, I had to do some research on the reason why Doris had attached herself to Cindy.

From what I have read, these are known as Spiritual Vampires: not like the vampires in films, that drain your blood; spiritual vampires need and drain your energy. Often, it is said that spirits like Doris are refusing to surrender to their own deaths.

Constant attachment can cause one's energy system to break down and can in extreme cases cause physical illness. This explains why I had felt ill for days after a few of my experiences. I was shocked to read somewhere recently that at least seventy-five percent of individuals have at one time or another suffered from this.

Having found this out, I feel I should inform people of both the dangers towards the likes of Cindy, who are connected with the dying, or the number of non-believers that are not seeing the light and choosing to attach.

The job I am doing means the world to me. I will never underestimate the importance of it, however, it is wrong for hospital managers and others not to be aware of the responsibility needed for the safety of both their staff and patients.

Since starting my diary, I have written things down that I can't remember writing, or that simply don't make sense to present-day events. The strongest entry in my diary that I can recall is that ripples can create tsunamis that knock down the mightiest of walls. It made no sense until now. I am reminded of the film, Jaws and how this film had the power to have such a lasting effect on people's fears. I am embarrassed to think that I could be capable of creating such an effect, but, that being said, I am convinced that someone needs to say something.

I know some of the church members are aware that I am writing a book. I have even had messages from mediums regarding this. One message that sticks in my mind was that I was told to stop making excuses for the reason why I couldn't write, such as wrong type of paper, wrong coloured pen and I was just asked to get on with it. Another message was from a medium. In her vision, she saw me standing in a cave, on the walls were carvings of past spiritual teachings on the walls. In my hand, I held a hammer, but no chisel. I didn't understand the meaning at the time. Maybe you can? I will give you my understanding of her message, later on.

I mentioned the circle in the north of England attended by my mother and sister, and how they stumbled upon crossings. Their church committee found out and questioned whether such spirits should be brought forward into the church. It breaks my heart that these people would question the need to help and decide to turn their backs on anyone, alive or dead, that may need help. I understand, more than most, the need for safety, but ignoring the problem doesn't make it go away.

We attend the church, not for proof, as we have that; we attend church both to learn to pass on proof to others, but also to find a way to make this earth a safe and beautiful place.

I thought sitting vigil was my job, my path. I am now convinced that more is involved. The mightiest of walls are the policies in the industry of death, Old people's homes, hospitals, hospices. If a spirit was a virus that could be attached to those that care for a patient, every care would be taken. Like a virus, a spirit cannot always be seen and yet both symptoms can be devastating to the victim.

My wish, hope and prayer for the future is that the work I am doing is accepted and that everyone calls upon a Spiritual Minister, as they do a Chaplain, but unlike the Chaplain, they need no faith, just love and guidance. One person, just one rippler cannot bring about this change. All I can do is ask you to continue the ripple, making it grow in strength. The rest is down to you, to inform everyone you can of the dangers.

Once many ripplers start to ask questions and ask for protection, for both themselves and their loved ones, leaders and managers will have to listen and act. Not only that, I believe that all churches, Spiritualist or other, need to address this. Pilot lights will be lit inside people, and they will want information, protection and knowledge.

Before I started this book, I was told that there would be nine ripplers. I wonder whilst writing this if the second rippler is the one that will spread the information and change in the churches.

CHAPTER 21: ENDING

*I*t has been months now since I have had any communication from my Guides, or any visions. Even my vigils at the hospital have become less frequent, as we have been blessed with more volunteers. Everything I have been shown or witnessed has gone into this book and as no more is forthcoming, I have to figure out the ending.

Since the start of Chapter One, I have told you that writing has never been a wish of mine. I have found it hard to understand why Spirit would ask me, the least likely person to do this book any justice.

Using my very practical brain, I can argue that, as I have no skills in writing, I cannot influence their meanings or messages or have the imagination to over exaggerate the truth.

On a personal level, it may well be a lesson to overcome my own fears of judgement. The fear of discovering my ability was overpowering, and the most frightening thing I have ever experienced in my life. This could be the reason, to find that one person who is going through this and let them know they are not alone; or better still, perhaps this book may lead to dedicated rescue circles within our churches. Hopefully, writing about different ways to pass someone over may be of use.

The other reason is the ripple effect, that is needed in our hospitals, hospices, and care homes; they must address the possibilities of earthbound spirits attaching to the living.

The one person, or the chance of the circles mentioned above, that I can reach, gives a good enough reason to write. The change that we might be able to bring about in the workplace will be a very important reason for the book as well. However, as important as they all are, I know I haven't hit on the main purpose, so, I will continue to write, allowing my thoughts to be free. If all goes well, I won't change anything, as I am going to trust that spirit will guide my pen. Here goes...

I, like many, was nothing more than an individual with no knowledge outside of my family and friends. I felt disconnected with the present and uncertain, fearful of the future, not only of our country, but of the world.

Although I always felt accountable for the results of my small efforts, I couldn't see how one person could change a divided society. I see the world now with a loss of direction.

For thousands of years, God has entrusted humanity to spread his word, to enlighten our lives and live with just a few goals: to love one another, reproduce and to create harmony and peace.

Sadly, humanity's best intentions have caused more harm than good. I do refer to all religions, all tainted by people. All the wars stem from religion, race, power, and politics. We are being shown that unless we make profound changes in our human consciousness, the future of the human race is at stake.

No longer do we live in the past. We must live and change for today, creating a better tomorrow. Spiritualism must become the old spokesperson, renewed. Spiritualism is the hope of humanity on our troubled planet, where we must breathe the beauty of love and create light. This choice, to make changes and to connect with our higher energy, will start to make us feel closer to the real beauty of existence.

Negativity and fears are the products of a hallucinatory mind, constantly re-living the negative past or dragging it with us into the future, robbing us of the energy to deal with today.

Fears are not a sign of weakness. We have good reason to be fearful as a nation. Without fears, we wouldn't be able to work to improve and prevent things from happening. However, and I wish to emphasize this, the incredible, profound problem that we have in all this, is the shadows that feed these thoughts and cause that fear to spread like a virus.

Is it possible for us to live in a perfect world? A world without war, pain, suffering or indifference? Many futuristic movies portray this, but in these, this was achieved either through strict enforcement, impulse-numbing injections or computers preventing crimes before they were committed. They achieved a world devoid of violence or evil, but at a cost: the cost of our freedom or free will.

Evil is real and plays a major part in creating shadows. I have been told throughout my experiences that our world is shadowed and that the shadows feed our negative minds, fears and wants. We have been told that our loved ones cause the shadows. It could not be any simpler: help rescue the trapped and the shadows will be removed, therefore allowing the light to be seen and to be felt by everyone.

Only in meditation do we block these shadows and feed our souls from the light. Our souls will never hurt another; it is not possible. Our hearts are our gateway to our souls. Live via your heart and your soul will shine; live via your thoughts, greed, power or negativity, and these will feast from the shadows.

I once was told that we attract like for like. I lived with this fear for most of my adult life, and believed it to be true. If spirits were present, I was very good at picking up a bad spirit: the reason for not developing my ability, as I was always afraid. Thanks to my Guides and one lady from the church, I was corrected, and told that only the light can remove the darkness. I can't tell you how relieved I was to hear this.

A wise person once told me that the Old Testament is a cruel one; it was depicting God's way of punishing sins. To correct this, and show us He can forgive, He gave us Jesus, who in my eyes was most definitely a spiritualist. If that is in the Bible, is it so hard to believe that God can change with the times?

Since dedicating my life to God, I have always known a change was coming, something big, and I am not alone in thinking this. I haven't been able to understand it until now. We can all wait, and see if the change is for the worst, at our peril. Or we can unite and create the change. One day on the News, we will see a new light, or a new atmosphere, and this will be our evidence that we are working in the right direction. That day came for me, the day I was brave enough to write about Mr Black.

It has shown me that unconditional love is the key. United, we can change things, and create a better world. If I am right and the words given to me are correct, darkness is not just from evil spirits, the beautiful trapped souls in this book have shown that they also block the light.

In my diary I wrote about ripplers. That made no sense to me at the time, but now it is clearer. Perhaps I am a rippler, and this book is powerful enough to fall into the hands of those that are faithful enough to help build a tsunami of faith to knock down the walls.

What are the walls? I see two. One is the acceptance that people who work with end of life patients may be in danger and need knowledge. The other is the biggest of all, the one that I strongly believe is the only answer we have been given: how in our lifetime, we can start to end all wars, and that is to remove the shadows that feed the minds of evil. Once the shadows are removed - and this is not going to be overnight unless all across the world, we spiritual believers combine to work together - then maybe, just maybe, we could as a nation enter a new light, a world where peace and love will outweigh the darkness.

Don't forget what one small rescue circle hundreds of miles away tried to do, and how they rescued hundreds, if not thousands, at a time. I believe my purpose in writing this book is to plead for more circles to be set up, hopefully in the safety of our spiritual churches or within the safety of like-minded spiritual groups.

I plead with you as an individual, to join me: to talk to your churches, to open your circles to doing God's work now; to make this change happen.

Going back to my vision of the caveman's cave mentioned in an earlier chapter, with the carvings that were hard to understand at the time. If you remember, I had a hammer in my hand, but no chisel. This now feels much more significant to me, as I feel that maybe it's not my writing that is of importance, but the remnants of old religious teachings on the walls, that need to be obliterated and rewritten. Alone, I don't have all the tools required to do this. I hope instead that you will join me to accomplish this task, and that this book comes into the hands of the leaders of the churches and they help to rewrite those outdated teachings.

I promise to continue my diary and write up the wonders of the miracles which I trust will follow. Another year from now, hopefully, I will have the most beautiful spiritual story to tell.

As for today, I am both relieved and excited that this book has come to an end. Before my journey began, my life, although complete physically, was empty of spiritual knowledge. I had not found my purpose. I have now been blessed, not only to discover it, but also to have the knowledge that by my doing so, many souls have been helped to find their peace. In my eyes, there is no greater form of giving than spiritual rescuing. It is the highest form of love that we can give to another.

In completing this book, a part of my job is done, and I pray that spirit will guide readers not only to read this but to create the tsunami, that allows others to join the spirit rescues and highlight the dangers, regarding the hospices and other care centres.

I will say goodbye for now, and I leave you with a compilation of spirit's plea:

"Never in such an unhealthy state, your world has needed or requested such a radical change. We have a universe of our beloved lost ones, a task so great that it shadows your world and dims our hearts. We are reaching out for help; little can be done by one alone.

Skilled workers, unaware of their abilities, are awakening to their destiny. A great deal of work is being put in place here, as we speak. Our plight is being answered by those that listen and new guides will bring forward those lost into your circles. Lightworkers far and wide must join in a united form.

Own your quest, and stand proud."

The End

Printed in Great Britain
by Amazon